From Me To You

By: A.C.

"From Me to You" By: A.C.
Copyright © 2012 By U-Pub
All Rights Reserved
ISBN: #0982693141

FORWARD

I like this book because it will make you think. The author is just an honest man and he is simply telling you what he did, what will work. He writes how he talks so that you will feel comfortable reading his message.

If I had to pick one thing that this man stresses, it would be that you have a choice to make. People can only influence you, but no one can make that choice for you. If you refuse to make the choice, you will *unknowingly* make it for the worse. Each day, every minute of the day, you have a choice, and it is up to you to choose the right. If you don't choose the right, the wrong choice is automatic.

H.G.

FROM ME TO YOU
TABLE OF CONTENTS

CHAPTER 1
CHANGE IS CHANGE

Think about this for a moment: When you were a kid and your parents had to move, whether you wanted to or not, you had to move with them. You had just gotten used to the place where you lived and made some new friends, and now you had to move clear across the country. You were about to move to a place that you knew absolutely nothing about; it was a little scary and it involved a big change on your part. Your friends could not come with you, although maybe they could visit once in a few years or maybe not.

I agree, moving to another place is hard and can be a bit scary at times. Coming from a family that moved twenty-one times in eighteen years it was very tough on a young boy. I got held back in school, not because of grades but because we moved half-way through the year. I made friends but lost track of them because of moving. I can't tell you how many schools I went to or how many times I started in a new school; I guess it was something like sixteen times because we moved back to the same place sometimes.

When I moved down to Oklahoma from Massachusetts I knew no one in the vicinity but I moved anyway, with a little apprehension. But when I arrived at my destination I was surprised at what I found; very soon I had many friends, knew my way around, and loved it. I was living in a small town in Massachusetts and I moved to Tulsa, a city with a population, then, of about 400,000.

Also, when you graduated from high school and went away to college, you had to do your own laundry, you had to buy your own food, sometimes, and you had to clean your own dorm room. Then after college you, maybe, got married and took on a whole different way of live. You got a good job in the carrier that you studied for. How many changes do you go through and not pay attention to? Now that you are about 30, 40, 50, or so on, you look back to when you were in grade school to high school moving every year and wonder how you got through it all. Change is hard, at the time, but it is necessary and it is the only constant in life.

I have talked to people of many different backgrounds who have told me, "I can't change." I remember hearing one guy say this on television, "God, change me." Well, there is a truth to what both of those statements are saying. You can't change *on your own*. But you know, by looking at your past, that change in your life is inevitable, but it's hard. And the more you resist, the harder it will seem and the more it may hurt.

You may look at your life and see that you need to change, you know that your life is going nowhere fast and without change you will die a stupid death. But even though you know that you need to change, you just don't have then desire to change, you're too comfortable where you are. "For God is working in you, giving you the desire and the power to do what pleases him," (Philippians 2:13 NLT). God is more than you can possibly think, He is working on you heart right now, even as you are reading this book, He is working on your heart and giving you the desire to do what you knew you needed to do for Him, but never wanted to.

CHANGE AND EXCHANGE

When a person decides to be born again and saved there will be a change. "Therefore, if anyone is in Christ, he is a new creation; the old has gone, the new has come!" (2 Corinthians 5:17 NIV). If that person claims that he is a sinner still, either he has been taught to misunderstand the word, to keep him down, or he really has never given himself to God (entered into Christ). Why did I say that? Truth be told, there will be an exchange (a trade off) and it is by the man's desire— the man who is being born again and saved. Just as that verse said, he is a *new* creation; a new creation is one that has never been before. So, if the man says that he is a sinner saved by grace, saved by grace meaning being born again and saved by God's gift of grace and by his confession, he is either lying blatantly or lying unknowingly; he can't be both.

When the man is confessing his faith that Jesus is Lord the first time to be saved he is expressing the desire to put away the past sinner mentality, the sinful life that he used to live, and take on the new mentality of a child of God, a child who wants to please his Father. This man is no longer a sinner, or a sinful man, he is now a newly created child who wants to grow and be pleasing to God.

There is one verse in the epistles that says that Paul, even after he was born again, was still a sinner. Folks, you got to understand that the original manuscript of the Bible was written in ancient Hebrew, Greek, and some Aramaic; it was also translated many times before the King James Version, or any other twentieth century version was translated. The verse is 1 Timothy 1:15 and the New International Version has it as,

"Here is a trustworthy saying that deserves full acceptance: Christ Jesus came into the world to save sinners—of whom I am the worst." (1 Timothy 1:15 NIV).

I do not say that a born true Christian never sins—temptation is in the world—but what I am saying is that a saved man is not a sinner anymore, he doesn't make a practice of living in sin. A medical doctor practices medicine or medical doctoring, A football player makes a practice of playing football, a lawyer makes a practice of the law, a gambler makes a practice of gambling; just so, a sinner makes a practice of sinning. These people in these professions are ready to do them at the drop of a hat; that's their mentality, it's the way they think. So, for that verse,

10

1 Timothy 1:15, I do not believe that in the original letter Paul was actually telling Timothy that even though he was a new creation he was still a sinner. Either that's true or Paul wrote 1 Corinthians after he wrote 1 Timothy and he learned more.

Do you love God? Do you fear God? You might say yes to both of those questions, as many people do without thinking. I just listened to a teacher teaching about the fear of the Lord and it made me think.

I've heard people say that if God wants a man to do something He will provide, *before hand*, what is needed to complete the job; and I'm sure you have heard the same. That comes from the verse that says that we are to count the cost. Well, counting the cost is a good idea, you should know what it will take to do the job, but that doesn't mean that you shouldn't start on the job before all the provision is in to finish.

I am a tither; I'm committed to the tithe. When I moved down to Tulsa, Oklahoma from Pittsfield, Massachusetts I left what I had up there and moved down with hardly anything. Yes, I knew what it would take to live in Tulsa but I didn't have it, it wasn't manifest yet. When I got to my apartment in Tulsa, God had some guys come and help me move in, my bills didn't come for two months, my dad called, out of the blue, and paid my first months rent, and someone from my church gave me money for food. God took care of me because I obeyed Him and stepped out on what He wanted me to do.

"'I tell you the truth,' Jesus replied, 'no one who has left home or brothers or sisters or mother or father or children or fields for me and the gospel will fail to receive a hundred times as much in this present age (homes, brothers, sisters, mothers, children and fields—and with them, persecutions) and in the age to come, eternal life,'" (Mark 10:29-30 NIV).

That means that if you give something or leave something for the work of the gospel you can expect a return; but don't try to put a time limit on God.

When God told my friend to get his books published some well meaning people told him that it shouldn't cost him anything. There are precious few publishers that will publish an unknown author free of charge. In other words, he had to take the step to obey God whether it's going to cost him anything or not, and He will recompense. All he needed to do was get the books published, he let God handle the rest; he'll just do what He tells him.

Jesus, God among us, said,

"Whoever believes and is baptized will be saved, but whoever does not believe will be condemned. And these signs will accompany those who believe: In my name they will drive out demons; they will speak in new tongues; they will pick up snakes with their hands; and when they drink deadly poison, it will not hurt them at all;

they will place their hands on sick people, and they will get well," (Mark 16:16-18 NIV).

Many people who say they love God try to discount this Scripture by saying that it was not in the original manuscript. They don't know; the original manuscript was written about 2000 years ago and is, most likely, destroyed now—of course, I am not talking about the Dead Sea Scrolls. And besides, even if that Scripture wasn't originally in there, John 14:12, John 8:31-32, 1 Corinthians 5:17 and others were. There is no viable excuse for not obeying God's written and spoken word. But, before you can obey God you need to know *for yourself* what He said, and that means you must do your own reading and studying of the Holy Bible, God's written Word.

Remember, if you are born again and saved through your faith filled confession then you have made up you mind and purposed in your heart to give up the sinful past—the sinner life style—and taken on the mentality of a child of God who, both, loves and fears—worships, respects and obeys—his Father, God *without the 'He owes me' idea*.

MY LIFE CHANGING EXPERIENCE

All through middle school and high school I was different. There were the intellectuals, the jocks, the nerds, the bullies, and then there was me. I was not one of them. So, naturally, I was singled out, I was ragged on like one of the nerds, but the nerds ragged on me also. Some of the jocks, actually, did not rag on me, but they didn't come to my aid either. Of all the bullies in my high school, and there were quite a few, there was one that stood out; even the other bullies were timid when they were around him.

In the first week of my senior year in high school I accepted Jesus as my Lord, and here is how that came about. My parents were arguing something fierce so I went out for a walk, I was wearing long jeans and a long sleeve cotton dress shirt, the temperature was 70°. In less than five minutes I walked back in the house and my dad said, "I thought you were going to walk around the block," our block was a mile around. I did, I jogged part of it and walked the rest, and I did not even break a sweat, go figure. But anyway, I was still upset that night so after dinner I hopped in my red convertible and drove to my friends house, I knew he was a Christian. As I pulled into the driveway I scratched his father's white BMW, later I found a big white scratch on my car but there was not even a red spot on his dad's car. Anyway, he didn't even console me, as I said I was upset. So, then I drove over to another friends house, he was also a Christian. As you

14

could probably tell, I was looking for Christ in my life. Well, he and his family were about to go to bed because he was leaving for ORU in Tulsa the next day, but they all stayed up and prayed me into the loving arms of my Lord, I accepted Jesus that night. I went there crying tears of sorrow and sadness, but the tears changed for sadness to tears of joy, and they soon cleared up.

The next Monday I went to school, not realizing any change in my life yet. A freshman went into the bays room, right next to the window where all the bullies hung out, and someone, I don't know who, said something derogative and the worst bully of the bully squad took as something said to him; so he followed the freshman in. Well, I went in too. This bully was beginning to give the freshman a whirly (dunking his head in a dirty toilet and flushing) At the time I did not know what came over me but I leaned against the cinderblock wall and said, "_____," called the bully by name, "leave him alone!" The bully let the boy go and started in my direction, I was standing against the wall that led out of the room. Well, I didn't move, although my legs were having close fellowship, I just smiled at him. He looked at me with a grimace on his face and with eyes wide, and walked out of the room; I never saw him again, although the school year had just begun. Later I realized that a big angel was standing there between me and the bully and said to him, "If you want to hurt him you're going to have to go through me."

Well, I got no thanks from that freshman but some of the bullies began being friendly toward me, outside of school, some would even walk me home. After being in the school for two years, my junior year I was in Texas, I actually began making some friends. Of course, some kids in the school still ragged on me and I didn't like it, but it wasn't as bad as before.

That seemed to be an isolated incident, that business with the bully. Nothing of major proportions really happened after that, I didn't really show any change in my life, until after college when I was living in Massachusetts. I went through college for a degree in Business and planned to specify in sales, the college boasted that after graduation they would help me find a job in my field. Well, they didn't, so I wound up as a security guard. I read the Bible, the New Testament, through and again because a security guard on the night shift is as boring as a stripped log. But I understood nothing of what I read, and the pastors that I went to didn't help me. I even went to a Bible fellowship group and they didn't help me either.

But when we moved up to Massachusetts I met some carpenters, both Christians. One asked me to go with him down to a crusade in Nanuet, New York, and I found out that salvation is a process, I was baptized in the Holy Spirit down in Nanuet, and I began to pray in other *unlearned* tongues.

When that happened all that I had read in the Bible began to come back to me, like a flood. That's when the real changes in my life started and that's when I began to grow.

Like Peter from the Bible, I accepted Jesus as Lord earlier on and for years nothing really happened in my life. But the Jesus said,

"Just know this, you shall be enveloped in power once you are baptized in the Holy Spirit. This must be by your acceptance because the Father will never force anything upon anyone. But when you have this power you will witness—represent and spread the good news— of me, starting at home then spreading out," (Acts 1:8 Steadfast in Honor).

So, a few days after I was baptized in the Holy Spirit I realized a calling upon my life to represent Jesus; and that's what I'm doing with all my heart.

CHAPTER 2
WHAT DO YOU THINK?

In truth, your words are going to affect and cause an effect in your life and the lives of people around you. But let's start by going deeper than your words, right to your thought pattern.

This is something that effects everyone no matter who they are. Just think about it; how many inmates are in prison because they *did not* go along with someone breaking the law? How many dope addicts, dealers, alcoholics, sex offenders … got into that mess purely by accident, didn't think about it, weren't tempted? Obviously they must have thought something, maybe they thought it would be fun. So, then they probably said something, they might have simply said, "Ok." By the way, a smile is a none verbal, "Ok," or a nod, or even a raised hand could be a none verbal agreement.

Now, your thoughts are controlled by you; but they are influenced by someone or something else, I call these influences, signs. A sign could be a TV ad that you happened to see, a radio ad, a book, a billboard; even wind could be a sign. But, still, you control what you think, and that gives you control over what you say.

You can see something happening and say, "No, stop that," and, depending upon majority vote, it might stop. I'm sure you have seen a bully beating up a skinny kid on the playground, and the skinny kid's friends would come around and tell the bully to stop. Well, if the kid's friends were bigger the bully might stop, or if there were more of them he might stop. But if there was no threat of punishment from the kid's friends the bully might not stop.

There are many books written about the power of words, positive speaking, and positive thinking. But reading them and agreeing with them is not enough; they are signs telling you what you could do with your thoughts and words, and they require action.

Myself, I was having a time when a piece of house equipment kept on failing to work. Every time it failed to work I would say, "Watch me fix it and have something else go wrong." So, every time I fixed it something else would break on it. Then I would say, "This thing keeps falling apart." Again, I fixed it then it would fall apart. Every time it fell apart I would reinforce the fact that it's not working.

Finally, I woke up to what I was doing; I was agreeing with it instead of getting it to agree with me. Let me explain; every time it broke I would agree that it would never work right. But I should have been altering my thoughts and my words to take control of the situation and get the thing to work. The way to control a situation is to get the situation to agree with you and not to lower yourself under the situation. I needed to control the situation and get that thing to work. In order to do that I had to take the upper hand and control my thoughts and words. Get the thing to obey me and not the other way around.

You might have thought that things can't obey or disobey, they just do what they are made to do. They just do what they are made to do; that is called obeying the manufacturer. If an air conditioner didn't cool the air, the motor didn't even work, would it be obeying the manufacturer, or what you bought it to do?

I had a disobedient car once, this was before I learned about controlling my thoughts and words. It only worked in reverse; so, I sold the disobedient car for parts.

TONGUE WARS

You have, I'm sure, noticed the direction that gas prices are going and have been going for the past 40 years. I'm using gas prices as an example, but this issue is not limited to any one thing. Some people want to blame president Obama or the president who is in office at the time; but he has nothing to do with gas prices, OPEC does. But it isn't even OPEC that is to blame for the rise in gas prices; although their greed does have something to do with it.

So, why do you think these things are happing? Why was it that a person would spend $10 to fill a tank in 1980 and to fill that same tank now it would cost upwards of $40? Everyone likes to blame someone else, like the president or the market, but who voted the president in and who runs the market?

It has to do with the attitudes of people, but it goes further than that. It all boils down to that wagging thing between you teeth, you know, that thing that has the taste buds. Actually, it has to do with your tongue, your lips, and your larynx.

You look at what is happening to gas prices and you say what has just happened instead of doing what Jesus did by saying what should happen. So, by saying what has happened you give it license to happen again and again, and on it goes.

When someone came or was brought to Jesus *to be* healed, what did Jesus *say*? No, not what did He do, but what did He *say*? Well, let's look,

"But when Jesus heard *it,* He answered him, saying, 'Do not be afraid; only believe, and she will be made well.'" (Luke 8:50 NKJV).

Many people have said this, maybe even you, "God is in control." If that were true there would be no sickness, no rising prices, no homes being destroyed, no wars, no … I need not go on. God doesn't cause these things. So, who does?

"God blessed them, and God said to them, 'Be fruitful, multiply, fill the earth, and subdue it. Rule the fish of the sea, the birds of the sky, and every creature that crawls on the earth.'" (Genesis 1:28 HCSB).

You might know the story about what happened, but you might not; so, I'll tell you what happened. Right then God gave Adam full control over the earth and everything in it; authority to rule (control). When Satan came in as the snake, he was able to deceive both the woman and *the man*; essentially he grabbed the control from man and people have had a hard time ever since. Then Jesus came and went down to hell, on Satan's turf, defeated him on his own turf, and got the authority to control back from him. But who did God give it to in the first place? HE GAVE IT TO MAN BECAUSE THAT'S WHERE HE WANTED IT. So, what do you think God wanted Jesus to do with it, the authority to control? God had Jesus return it to where God had given it in the beginning, give it to man! When Jesus came back from the grave He said, "All authority..." (Matthew 28:18), essentially He was saying, "I'm in control..." or "I have to keys." But then He turned to Peter and the guys and tossed those keys to them/us.

Now *we* have the authority to control. But, ya know why it seems that we don't have control, and situations seem to be going wrong? Because we, you in particular, need to learn how to control your tongue to say the things that will bring a positive effect.

As I was talking to some good friends of mine I mentioned that if all the Christians in America, and everywhere else, got in agreement and said the same thing about gas prices, that they are coming down, by the end of this year they would be at $1.00 and coming down even further.

But, the way it seems right now, the way it *should not* be, is that there is a war in the body of Christ; and the reason is because some people speak according to what their physical senses pick up and some speak according to what Jesus wants to happen. Some people see what gas prices, food prices and so forth are doing and speak based upon what they have been doing in the past, and then when someone comes along and calls things that be not as though they were (Romans 4:17), they call him bad names and think he's lying. But if they would join him instead of ridiculing him they would, eventually, see great things. And if we all got together speaking the way God wants then we could win the tongue wars and see gas prices and other prices drop considerably.

CHANGE YOUR DESTINY

Some people believe that their words are from their thoughts and influenced by themselves. Businesses put out signs, billboards and advertisements to try to grab their attention, but no one influences their words accept themselves. Well, that's a pigheaded attitude and a false belief. You know what they're, unknowingly doing, don't you? They're saying what the devil wants them to say.

Other's believe that God is not in the picture and it is only them against the devil. So, the words that they speak are theirs because, "I ain't gonna listen to no devil, and I certainly don't agree with him." They're saying what the devil wants them to say also, not knowing that the devil is behind the words they're saying.

Then there are some who believe that God killed the devil—maybe wishful thinking—so they think that all the words they speak must be from God. They might get 'lucky' and say something that God wants them to say. But that God killed the devil is a lie. That goes right along with the phrase, "God is in control." I heard a song once that depicted Satan speaking, he was saying that when people think he is dead they will blame God for all the terrible things that he does, that would include the bad words that they speak.

Some believe that there are three sources of thoughts; there is God, there is Satan and then there is man. That's a very prideful belief. Is man the creator? Is man the corrupter? There is the family of God and there is the family of Satan; of which one are you?

Then there are more crazy people who know that God is alive, the devil is alive, but their words are from God, all the time, because they are Christians—so they say. God speaks through people, He has spoken through a donkey, but there is absolutely no one on earth today whom God speaks through at every minute of every day. The *one man*, Jesus, is still here by His Spirit, but not as *one man* anymore.

Now, there are also people who believe that angels speak to them and possibly even preach to them.

There is no evidence in the Bible that says anything about angels preaching the gospel.

"But even if we or an angel from heaven should preach to you a gospel contrary to *and* different from that which we preached to you, let him be accursed (anathema, devoted to destruction, doomed to eternal punishment)!" (Galatians 1:8 AMP).

So, there is one place were angels are referred to as *possibly* preaching, but even that isn't clear. God has many people around the world whom He wants to use to preach, and some are obedient enough to do the job. So, why is man doing the preaching?

"Then God said, 'Let Us make man in Our image, according to Our likeness. They will rule the fish of the sea, the birds of the sky, the livestock, all the earth, and the creatures that crawl on the earth.'" (Genesis 1:26 HCSB).

We are the ones with control, that's why we are the ones whom God has chosen to preach. But now, God has given His words and the devil has given his words. Now, the decision is yours: whose words are you going to agree with? One way that you agree with words is by putting them in your mouth and speaking them. Another way to agree with words is by thinking along with them, which will eventually send them out your mouth, so you speak them.

"How can people have faith in the Lord and ask him to save them, if they have never heard about him? And how can they hear, unless someone tells them? And how can anyone tell them without being sent by the Lord? The Scriptures say it is a beautiful sight to see even the feet of someone coming to preach the good news," (Romans 10:15-15 CEV).

When he wrote, "And how can anyone tell them without being sent by the Lord?" the apostle Paul was talking about someone who is honestly sent by God to bring you the truth. There are many, many, boocoos of people who will come to you preaching non-sense, but not that many who are truly sent to bring you the truth. If anyone comes to you claiming that what they are saying is gospel truth, ask them what scripture they can show you to back it up.

READING OUT LOUD

Now, this is something that I learn to do when I was in a hospital a while ago. I had a Bible and I read it in silence but, "No one can have faith without hearing the message about Christ." (Romans 10:17 CEV); that is faith in Christ. I did have some visitors, but they didn't tell me anything of truth about Jesus and God's love. So, I had to preach to myself, out loud; that is when I started reading the Bible out loud to myself. It is a good practice to get into. But when you are reading out loud to yourself you are making a confession of agreement, so you want to stay away for reading negative things out loud.

When I am reading out loud I am in agreement with what I am reading, so I don't read everything out loud, because not everything is healthy for me to agree with; I don't want the negatives in my life. And when I agree with something, by confessing it, I am allowing it to effect my life.

When you go to a restaurant, a very nice place, and the waiter comes to takes your order; do you read off everything on the menu out loud, or do you just read him what you want to eat? Well, in the same way, when you read a book to yourself (you being the waiter), you don't have to read the whole book (the menu) out loud, but only what you want to eat. In Proverbs 18:21 the tongue means your words (words off the menu), those who love it are those who use their tongues (read the menu out loud), and they will eat its fruit (what you have read out loud). "The tongue has the power of life and death, and those who love it will eat its fruit." (Proverbs 18:21 NIV).

CHAPTER 3
THE CHOICE IS YOURS

You have a choice in the matter. Even if someone held you at gun point and told you that you had to spit in the eye of your wife or they would kill you; you could always choose death.

Suppose you had two dishes served to you, one was piled high with poisonous roots, dead snakes, live spiders (that you had to swallow whole), and bird droppings; the other dish had some food that you knew you made you sick. You are starving, you hadn't eaten in forty days. Well, the choice is your, what are you going to do?

Suppose you are blindfolded and sitting in the middle of a room. There is a time bomb in the room and you can hear it ticking loudly, but you don't know when it will go off, it could go off any minute now. You have to get out of that room as fast as you can but the walls have been electrified and your hands are bond behind your back. Your legs are free but there is a huge hole right in front of you. If you were to fall through that hole you would find yourself in an endless fall, scraping the sides of *I'll not mention it* until you go splat. If you don't move you will go out with a bang.

You hear a man walking in the room and it is evident that he is not bound or blindfolded and it's pretty clear that he knows where the exit is. Now you have three choices, you can either go out with a bang—the bomb, which is living a mediocre life, going to church or belonging to a denomination and thinking that will get you the heaven; you can go splat—the fall, which is staying away from church 'because of the hypocrites.'; or you can *politely* ask for this man's help and he will bring you safely out.

You are right, there is a catch. If you ask the man for his help he will help you, but you will have to do it his way.

Nobody in their right mind wants to go to hell. In that room with the bomb are the three choices for your eternal life. Will it be splat, bang, life in hell; or a love-life in heaven, which is true life? The room represents your life on earth and there is a time bomb that's going to destroy it. But when is the bomb going to go off? You don't know the answer to the question because you didn't set it so quit thinking you have time. It could be that that time will come before you finish reading this book. "But, I feel fine," someone might say. That doesn't matter. The bomb will go off anyway, and the bomb is always with you, but it doesn't have to mean the end of everything.

My friend wrote a book about the subject of now. In it he brought out the fact that later is not born yet. What happens later, if there is a later, depends upon what you do now, not what you did in the past.

So right now come to Jesus, accept him as your personal Savior and Lord. Here's how, speak this prayer out loud with your mouth and pray it in you heart:

Oh, did you know that God actually raised Jesus from the dead for you? Believe it! When I prayed and was saved I had to purposely believe that for a while until I understood it.

Dear God, in Jesus' name,

I now realize that my life has been getting me nowhere, nowhere in truth.

I realize that it is only with Jesus the Christ that I can be a winner, and I want to win.

What the writer said is true, I don't know when the bomb will go off and I don't want to go to hell.

I'm declaring Jesus the Christ as my personal Savior and Lord now and I repent of sin.

I'm going to get a Bible and read it to find out what you want me to do, I don't want to be a hypocrite.

Thank you, Jesus, for saving me

and showing me how to get to heaven.

OBEDIENCE

That seems to be a word that has lost it's meaning in most of the churches today. Many people have read that the works that God requires is that we believe on the name of Jesus and so that is what they do, *they think*. But Jesus went on to explain what it means to believe. Many who call themselves Christians think of believing in Jesus as sitting back and letting Him do all the work and agreeing that He is able to do anything. But what did Jesus say that believing in Him is? Jesus said,

"I tell you the truth, anyone who believes in me will do the same works I have done, and even greater works, because I am going to be with the Father," (John 14:12 NLV).

To do what Jesus told us to do is to be obedient. Remember, this verse is still very much alive today, "If you are willing and obedient, you will eat the best from the land;" (Isaiah 1:19 NIV).

You might look at that and see the next verse about refusing and rebelling and think, '*So, rebelling must be the opposite of being obedient. Well, I'm not rebelling so I must be obedient.*' You're making me laugh.

No, that's giving the two extremes: or is it? So, your thought should be: '*Am I truly being obedient or is there some rebellion in my heart that I am not aware of?*' It's pretty obvious that if you are not willing then you are refusing. And, I guess, refusing to be obedient to do something that Jesus did is being rebellious.

Now, Jesus gave a command, not a suggestion, that His born again disciples "Receive the Holy Spirit," (John 20:22). But many people say, "Since I confessed

Jesus as Lord I automatically have the Holy Spirit." But, that is an ignorant lie because there are certain attributes that come with the Holy Spirit; there is evidence that will be apparent.

When Jesus said, "I am in the Father and the Father is in me" (John 14:11) He was talking about the baptism in the Holy Spirit of God (the Father). Jesus came from the Father, He is the Son of God born of the Holy Spirit (the fruit of the Spirit), and He was also anointed (baptized) in the Holy Spirit (the Father). So, Jesus had the Holy Spirit in Him (the Father's blood runs through the Sons veins) and He was anointed in the Holy Spirit. He did this and then told us,

"I assure you: The one who believes in Me will also do the works that I do. And he will do even greater works than these, because I am going to the Father," (John 14:12 HCSB).

Now, that is the second thing that a person who is serious about going to heaven must do, if they live more than a day, and if they hear about the Holy Spirit. But that is not an excuse for thinking, '*Well, ok, I'm set now. Now I can relax.*' I sincerely hope you're joking. No, there are certain things that I call earmarks of a true Christian. You can't do them until you are in the Father (baptized in the Holy Spirit). Jesus did them all and then He told us to do them; they are listed in Mark 16:17-18. Sure it's God who does the works but you are supposed to be in the Father

(Holy Spirit) by way of the baptism; He wants to work through you and me. There are four words that I would add to verses 17-18 just to alleviate confusion, they are WHEN THE NEED ARRISES.

If you find something in the Bible that Jesus said to do but your church doesn't teach it or you don't know if you should do it, I suggest that you pray about it because the translation may be off; but it *could be* that your church is wrong. If someone tells you that God wants you to do something and it is not directly backed up in Scripture, I suggest you put that idea on the back burner and pray about it. If it's right you will get confirmation, a verse will back it, and God will give you a word of "Go ahead" for it; and if it is wrong for you, you won't get a "Go ahead" from God. Or, if a Bible verse, Jesus, tells you that you should do something, but your church friends tell you that only Jesus could do that and you can't, pray about it and for your church friends because they are very possibly wrong.

THE HOLY SPIRIT BAPTISM

"Receive the Holy Spirit," Jesus said that in John 20:22 (almost every version or translation of the Bible). Most 'Christians' take that to mean get born again and saved, and they *automatically* believe that when a person accepts that Jesus is Lord, he or she receives the Holy Spirit. My friends, this is not sound according to Bible Scripture; it's based on man's idea. I find no Bible verses that say that when a man accepts Jesus as Lord the Holy Spirit comes into him. Now, there is one place in the Bible that tells us that we have the fruit of the Spirit, but that still doesn't say that the Holy Spirit comes in us, that verse is Luke 1:35 (look it up).

Okay now, Jesus told you to receive the Holy Spirit, Paul calls this action the baptism in the Holy Spirit and so did John the baptizer,

"I baptize you with water to show that your hearts and lives have changed. But there is one coming after me who is greater than I am, whose sandals I am not good enough to carry. He will baptize you with the Holy Spirit and fire," (Matthew 3:11 NCV).

And, since the believer will speak in other, new tongues (Mark 16:17), tongues that the natural world does not and cannot speak in, and this supernatural language (tongues) comes with the baptism in the Holy Spirit; well, it sounds like this baptism is needed.

"And these signs will accompany those who believe: In my name they will drive out demons; they will speak in new tongues;" (Mark 16:17 NIV). I believe that this kind of tongues is for prayer.

I'm not here to tell you what the Lord told me about this baptism, I'm here to make you think.

Many people call themselves Christians and; well, in truth they are children of God because of their confession of Jesus. But that confession, don't throw stones, does not *automatically* make anyone a Christian. If you want to argue that point, and I know many of you do, you will have to, first, learn why those at Antioch called the disciples Christians. The word **christ** means anointed one; anointed with what or whom? Who was Jesus anointed with?

"You know that God anointed Jesus from Nazareth with the Holy Spirit and with power. Jesus went everywhere and did good things, such as healing everyone who was under the devil's power. Jesus did these things because God was with him," (Acts 10:38 GW).

By the way, the word **anointed** and the word **baptized** mean basically the same thing—to be smeared over or immersed in. Now, Jesus was anointed or baptized in the Holy Spirit; so what did Jesus do to show it? He went around healing the sick, virtually beating up the devil. Why? Because God (the Holy God who is the Spirit)-the Holy Spirit-was with Him.

"But if I do them, even though you do not believe me, believe the works, that you may know and understand that the Father is in me, and I in the Father," (John 10:38 NIV).

Note the last 9 words, "the Father is in me, and *I in the Father*." When you get bon again by your faith filled confession that Jesus is Lord, Jesus-the Father-is in you, possibly; He is given to you. I heard a radio announcer say, "Give yourself to God." When you give yourself to God by being baptized in the Holy Spirit (God's Spirit; God) you are in the Father-the Holy Spirit.

Then you have, not only the authority but the demonstration, power to 'kick the devil's butt' by,

"And these signs will accompany those who believe: In my name they will drive out demons; they will speak in new tongues; they will pick up snakes with their hands; and when they drink deadly poison, it will not hurt them at all; they will place their hands on sick people, and they will get well, " (Mark 16:17-18 NIV).

By the way, I wouldn't go around picking up deadly snakes or drinking poison if you don't have to just to prove that you are a Christian; you don't want to tempt God, even Jesus wouldn't do that.

Jesus is coming to Earth to retrieve His own. Does that mean all those who think they are Christians because they have, at one time, confessed Jesus as Lord and who go to church, or does it mean He is coming for His representatives?

"But you will receive power when the Holy Spirit comes on you; and you will be my witnesses in Jerusalem, and in all Judea and Samaria, and to the ends of the earth," (Acts 1:8 NIV).

A better rendering of the word for witness is representative. A representative of the army sounds and does the army; he lives the army everywhere he goes. To all those around him he is the army. Just so, a representative of Jesus, one whom the Holy Spirit is on, sounds and does Jesus; he is Jesus to all those around him. Jesus was baptized in the Holy Spirit (in God); are you?

WHAT DID JESUS DO?

"I tell you the truth, anyone who has faith in me will do what I have been doing. He will do even greater things than these, because I am going to the Father," (John 14:12 NIV).

This brings up the title question; *what* did he do—that we should do? Some would jump to the conclusion, "Well, Jesus preached to the multitudes, and that's what we should do." That is one thing that He did, but it is only one thing. When Jesus began his ministry what did He do? Well, He went to be baptized in water and when He came up—so baptism in water must mean that He was submerged—God baptized Him in the Holy Spirit, He received it.

"When He had been baptized, Jesus came up immediately from the water; and behold, the heavens were opened to Him, and He (John) saw the Spirit of God descending like a dove and alighting upon Him," (Matthew 3:16 NKJV).

So, Jesus was baptized in water and the Holy Spirit—He must have spoken in tongues because that is the primary physical evidence of the Holy Spirit baptism. The first recorded miracle accredited to Jesus was turning the water into wine at Cana, so let's look at that.

"On the third day a wedding took place at Cana in Galilee. Jesus' mother was there, and Jesus and his disciples had also been invited to the wedding. When the wine was gone, Jesus' mother said to him, 'They have no more wine.' 'Dear woman, why do you involve me?' Jesus replied. 'My time has not yet come.' His mother said to the servants, '<u>Do whatever he tells you</u>.' Nearby

41

stood six stone water jars, the kind used by the Jews for ceremonial washing, each holding from twenty to thirty gallons. Jesus said to the servants, 'Fill the jars with water'; so they filled them to the brim. Then he told them, 'Now draw some out and take it to the master of the banquet.' **They did so**," (John 2:1-8 NIV).

Notice the underline part and what is in boldface, there is a definite meaning. This miracle was credited to Jesus' ministry, but was it **only** Jesus who did something? Jesus had a good control over His words, and Mary knew that, she knew His words worked. But then the servants did what He said, they obeyed. I've talked to people who don't believe that their words have anything to do with their lives; Jesus prophesied his death and resurrection at least three times and it happened.

Jesus cast out demons because they didn't belong where they were; they were possessing people who, obviously, didn't want them. Demons sap life out of people, they use those people to cause trouble, mislead others, and everything evil (but not all at once, they are deceptive). Demons know the authority of the name of Jesus and the power of the Holy Spirit.

"What do you want with us, Jesus of Nazareth? Have you come to destroy us? I know who you are—the Holy One of God!" (Mark 1:24 NIV).

When you use the name of Jesus, demons must

42

obey; if they don't the Holy Spirit of God will whip their behinds to the front.

Jesus healed the sick, cleansed the lepers, made the lame to walk, lifted the paralyzed from their mats, restored sight to the blind (both physically and spiritually), made the mute to speak, opened deaf ears; and what else? Oh yes, He taught truth. Yes, He was gentle, but He was also straight forward.

"Woe to you, teachers of the law and Pharisees, you hypocrites! You travel over land and sea to win a single convert, and when he becomes one, you make him twice as much a son of hell as you are." (Matthew 23:15 NIV).

Some might think that Jesus pronounce these woes while He was sitting with His friends and the Pharisees and Scribes weren't there. I believe they were right there and He was telling them *like it is*. I believe there must have been Pharisees and teachers of the law in the crowds that hung around Jesus because they were watching Him to catch Him in a fault so that they could put Him to death. If you will look at the first verse of the very next chapter you will find out that He was saying all these things, pronouncing these woes, while he was sitting in the temple; some Pharisees are always at the temple.

So, what did the Pharisees represent? They represented religion, not being a little christ. Everything the law—not the Ten Commandments, but the man made

43

law of religious legalism—said, the Pharisees represented with plenty of pride. Jesus represented a free life of God's love, and that was against their legalistic ideas.

Yes, Jesus did love all people, fact is, He died for us all; but He hated sin with a passion because sin is corrosive to life. He was always gentle and *Godly* wise when dealing with sin.

"and said to Jesus, 'Teacher, this woman was caught in the act of adultery. In the Law Moses commanded us to stone such women. Now what do you say?' They were using this question as a trap, in order to have a basis for accusing him. But Jesus bent down and started to write on the ground with his finger. When they kept on questioning him, he straightened up and said to them, '**If any one of you is without sin, let him be the first to throw a stone at her**,'" (John 8:4-7 NIV).

The only thing that Jesus did that you do not have to do is die on a cross. Why is that, as if you didn't know? Well, no matter how good you are and how much you love everyone in the world, you cannot take the sins of the whole world on your back and die for them. It just wouldn't work, and it's also not necessary because that was a once for all deal. Healing the sick, casting out demons, giving to the poor, all the rest of that stuff; those are not things that He did once to one person and is done for all. He wants you to continue His work.

When you give to one poor man, does that mean there are no more poor men in the world? What about the sick, you heal one; are there any more? You cast a demon out of one man, how many others may be demon possessed or oppressed? What are you going to do about speaking in tongues?

So, what will you do, aside from being a pastor, evangelist, teacher, prophet, apostle, or whatever other personal calling there is?

In the book of Acts, Luke wrote about the continuation of what Jesus had started, "In my first book I told you, Theophilus, about everything Jesus began to do and teach," (Acts 1:1 NLV). Look at something that Peter and John, *ordinary men*, did,

"But Peter said, 'I don't have any silver or gold! But I will give you what I do have. In the name of Jesus Christ from Nazareth, get up and start walking.' Peter then took him by the right hand and helped him up. At once the man's feet and ankles became strong," (Acts 3:6-7 CEV).

I've heard people say that healing the sick by faith went out with the apostles. Where did that come from? God's word says, "Jesus Christ is the same yesterday, today, and forever, (Hebrews 13:8 HCSB). Jesus is the personified word of God, so if He doesn't change then God's word doesn't change. And, if you will look in the American dictionary you will find that God's word is His will. So, if His word doesn't change then His will doesn't change. And if His will was healing then, then healing is His will today. Besides that, apostle are just men like you and me.

CHAPTER 4
THE CHOICE IS YOURS

Still, the choice is yours. If you decide to do what I have written, what the Bible has written, I will tell you more about this new life as a Christian; it depends more upon you than most people will tell you, and that's only because they don't know, have been misled, or have not studied specifically. If you choose not to obey Jesus and the word I will tell you a little about what you are in for, it's not pretty.

BE A REPRESENTATIVE

Many of you *think* you know. You *think* that because you have confessed Jesus as Lord you are saved and that makes you a Christian. But, did you know that not everyone in Paul's time who confessed Jesus as Lord were Christians? Case it point,

"It happened that while Apollos was at Corinth, Paul passed through the upper country and came to Ephesus, and found some disciples. He said to them, 'Did you receive the Holy Spirit when you believed?' And they *said* to him, 'No, we have not even heard whether there is a Holy Spirit.' And he said, 'Into what then were you baptized?' And they said, 'Into John's baptism.'" (Acts 19:1-3 NASB).

These 'disciples' were believers in Jesus because of the preaching of John the baptizer. They were baptized in water; they believed in Jesus, I'm sure they confessed Jesus as Lord. But,

"Then Jesus turned to the Jews who had claimed to believe in him. 'If you stick with this, living out what I tell you, you are my disciples for sure. Then you will experience for yourselves the truth, and the truth will free you,'" (John 8:31-32 MSG).

In that passage, take the words **the Jews** out and replace them with your name, because Jesus is talking to you. I used The Message Bible because it clears up the fact that listening to the word preached is not enough, you have to do it and don't give up if you don't see results right away. The truth is God's word, and Jesus is giving you God's word; so, that is what He means for you to be doing; that's why when you are doing it you will be experiencing the truth. Then Jesus said,

"I tell you the truth, anyone who believes in me will do the same works I have done, and even greater works, because I am going to be with the Father." (John 14:12 NLT) (Read verses around it).

Now, what did Jesus do while he was on the earth, as one man? Oh, by the way; a true believer, as Jesus said in Acts 1:8, is meant to be a witness (a representative) of Jesus after the Holy Spirit comes on him. So again, what did Jesus do? Was Jesus of Nazareth baptized in the Holy Spirit (the word used is anointed)? According to Peter, in Acts 10:38, He was and He went around doing good *and healing all who were oppressed.* Was Jesus anointed with the Holy Spirit from birth? According to Matthew 3:16 He wasn't.

By the way, the word **christ** means anointed, not *The* anointed, that's when it is referring the Jesus. I remember a preacher praying in the name of christ. I asked him whose name he meant? Anyone who is anointed with the Holy Spirit is a christ child (little christ). Christ is not a last name, or any name for that matter.

"So," you might ask, "to be a Christian you have to be anointed or baptized in the Holy Spirit. Is that what you are saying?" Well, you do need to be baptized (anointed) in the Holy Spirit, yes, and that will make you a little christ. But, that still doesn't mean that you are an acting Christian, it means that you are closer and you should continue.

Before I explain that any further let me quote to you a very important verse from Acts, a verse that not many people pay much attention to, "and when he found him, he brought him to Antioch. So for a whole year Barnabas and Saul met with the church and taught great numbers of people. *The disciples were called Christians first at Antioch*," (Acts 11:26 NIV).

Why were the disciples, those who stuck with Jesus' word and were living it out, called Christians at Antioch? In Acts 1:8 Jesus told the disciples that they would be anointed with the Holy Spirit *if they waited for Him* and then they would be His representatives (the word **witnesses** means representatives, here). What does a representative do? Well, a representative of America (an ambassador) is educated to be America to the country he goes to. Meaning, if you are talking to him you are talking to America. He does what America does. That is why not just anyone who lives in America is a good ambassador (representative) for America.

Now, after Jesus was baptized (anointed) in the Holy Spirit, what did He do? Did Jesus cast out demons, not just out of people but wherever necessary? Did Jesus lay hands on the sick? Did He pray in tongues, as an effect of this baptism?

He is *the* Christ. A Christian, according to the Bible, according to those in Antioch, is one who emulates *the* Christ, is a christ one or a representative in action of *the* Christ.

If you read this and find, after looking at your own life and belief system, that you are not really a Christian, but you thought you were, don't be embarrassed. Why, don't be embarrassed? Because there are many, many people who fall into that category. Now, let's correct the problem. Be baptized in the Holy Spirit; all you need to do is ask Jesus to baptize you and open your mouth, give control over your tongue to the Holy Spirit; feel free to sound ridiculous. This is called speaking in tongues and it's supernaturally normal. No one, on earth, will understand you; but that's alright because you aren't speaking to anyone on earth. Then read the Gospels and find out what Jesus did to show God's love; and do the same.

Just because it was done once by Jesus doesn't mean it doesn't have to be continued by you.

RAPTURE

Yes, I know the word **rapture** is not in the Bible, the term caught up is. But when the Christian thinks of being caught up to heaven the sense of joy is unspeakable, that is what **rapture** means, it's a synonym.

Who goes in the rapture? Everyone who claims that Jesus is Lord thinks that he or she is going, but that's not true. What did Jesus say? "Why do you call me Lord, Lord and do not do what I say," (Luke 6:46 NIV).

Some people seem to think that means what Paul said in Romans 10:9-10; it doesn't. Others think it means pray and ask Him for things; that's only a part of what Jesus said to do. What did Jesus say that those who believed will do? Well, before I get into that, would Jesus tell His beloved to do something that he didn't do? He is a success, is He not? And when a successful person is telling you how to be a success, would he tell you to do something other than what he did? So, Jesus must have done what he told us to do. Now, why would He tell you to do something that He knew you couldn't do? He said,

"Very truly I tell you, whoever believes in me will do the works I have been doing, ad they will do even greater works than these, because I am going to the Father," (John 14:12 NIV).

So, the next question you've got to ask yourself is, what did Jesus do? Some versions of John 14:12 actually say that the one who believes can do ... Well, that would mean that if the need was present before you and you could meet that need then you would because you believe in Jesus, right? So, do you meet that need?

Am I being tough on you? If I am it's only because I want to see you in heaven and the signs of the times are very clear, the time is near.

Jesus also spoke of some things that would indicate a true believer; I guess it would show the difference between a ready for heaven believer and one
52

who is not ready for heaven or just wants to make people think he is a believer.

"And these signs will accompany those who believe: In my name they will drive out demons; they will speak I new *unlearned* tongues; they will pick up snakes *if necessary* with their hands ... ; they will place their hands on sick people, and they will get better," (Mark 16:16-18 NIV *italic inserted for clarity*).

People have argued that some earlier versions exclude these verses, but they're also covered in John 14:12. Some people might argue that Jesus didn't speak in tongues. Acts 10:38 tells us that Jesus was anointed (baptized) with the Holy Spirit, and Romans 8:26 tells us about the Holy Spirit praying through us with groanings. At the tomb of Lazarus Jesus groaned in the Spirit and the in verse 41 He said "Father, I thank you that you already heard me." O, He must have spoken in tongues.

Now, what does Mark 16:16-17 say about you? What should you do?

So, if you are in obedience to the Lord Jesus, do what He did, and then doing the more that He tells you to do; that doesn't mean that you must go around looking for sick people to lay hands on, looking for demon possessed people to cast the demon out, looking for snakes to pick up; just be ready to do those things when the need arises. And if you are in obedience when Jesus comes to take the church home then you will be going with Him.

HELL IS ALL IT'S CRACKED UP TO BE

Believe it or not, some people actually want to go to hell. I don't know why, I guess they think it must be fun. They're probably thinking, '*Man, I can get high all the time and there will be no cops to say that I'm braking the law. Hey, I won't go to jail, jail's a drag. Hey, and we can all have a blast, just drinkin' and druggin' and, hey, the babes. Man, I can have sex all the time, non-stop. . . And when I get tied of that then I can leave.*' They probably think that doing all that 'good' stuff here is fun but, so it hurts some people.

But there are a few things wrong with that train of thought. The beginning, the middle, and the end; totally wrong! I mean, whoever sold them that bill of goods got away with murder, and I mean double edged, bloody murder!

Now, I know that you're not like that, you know better than to believe a lie like that, you know that hell is no party. But for those who don't know or don't realize it let me give you an illustration. Imagine yourself having the flu. You don't like having the flu do you? Its bad, you ach, you really don't want company; you just want to go to bed. Well now, imagine that you have the flu ten thousand times worse. Not only do you have that terror but you also have every other disease known to man, and your insides are falling out. On top of that, you are laying down on top of a sheet of dry ice (dry ice burns and eats away flesh) and you can't get off. Add to that, there is dry ice all around you touching every part of your body. You *really* don't want to see anyone and you *really* don't want anyone to see you. This is **BAD!** (with a capital B) to put it mildly.

Jesus said, "And throw the good-for-nothing servant into the outer darkness; there will be weeping and grinding of teeth," (Matthew 25:30 AMP).

And, "And if your hand causes your downfall, cut it off. It is better for you to enter life maimed than to have two hands and go to hell—the unquenchable fire, [where Their worm does not die, and the fire is not quenched.]" (Mark 9:43-44 HCSB).

Do you feel like you want to go there now, knowing that this is what you're in for? I'm sure you know what it's like in plane crashes; I know you've heard reports and seen it on TV. Well, imagine yourself in a plane crash but with all of that other stuff too, the dry ice and all that disease. And what's worse is that it is not a one time thing, it's a continual deal, it happens every second of every day, and you exist through it. Now, there's more. I know that if you could, being in this situation, you'd probably be thinking, '*I can't get out of this mess until I die.*' But, no, you can't die. Remember, you are not on earth anymore. If you were, you could die and get out of this mess. But this is hell where you will spend eternity. So you can't die and get out of this mess.

And all the drugs on earth and the alcohol that's on earth is not in hell—maybe for fuel—only the people who didn't repent and turn their lives around are. Though you are out of your natural earthly body you still have your feelings, and it **huuuurrrts**, oh boy does it ever hurt.

Now, with all off that going on do you still want to find a nice pretty babe to have sex with, as if sex were something that you could do in hell? Remember, you are no longer in your earthly body anymore and that's where the sex parts were. Would you like to know who is going to help you, give you some relief or good feeling amidst all that mess? I'll tell you. NO ONE! No one cares what's going on with you because they are in the same kind of situations.

Oh, there's one other thing but it doesn't help the poor dilapidated situation you're in. The one more thing is that you have absolutely no power. You might think that means that you can't get out of that situation, which you can't, but that's already been established. No, I mean you have no power at all; you can't even bat an eyelash, so-to-speak. You think you can blink? Forget it, you can't. So your eyes burn also.

Now, how many of you want to go to hell? I didn't think so. NO! Ya see, you're smart enough to know that that would not be fun, no pleasure at all. So, are you ready to take the step to avoid that kind of eternal punishment? Okay, all you need to do is accept Jesus Christ as your Lord and Savior. That's not hard, is it?

You, probably, know by now that I am a Christian and you're right. I am not ashamed of the Gospel of truth. One day a while ago I asked that Lord to give me a revelation of hell so that I could tell it to you. You know He won't send anyone to hell, even for a revelation. No, people send themselves to hell by not accepting God's One path to heaven. Anyway, what He did was revealed to me, through His Word, what hell is like. It is written that in hell, or utter darkness, there is weeping and gnashing of teeth and this is why.

Now, for you who are smart enough to want to stay away from all that mess I will give you a prayer to pray, out loud and in your heart:

Dear God, in Jesus' name,

I now realize that my life has been getting me nowhere, nowhere in truth.

I realize that it is only with Jesus the Christ that I can be a winner, and I want to win.

What the writer said is true, I don't know when the bomb will go off and I don't want to go to hell.

I'm declaring Jesus the Christ as my personal Savior and Lord now and I repent of sin.

I'm going to get a Bible and read it to find out what you want me to do, I don't want to be a hypocrite.

Thank you, Jesus, for saving me
and showing me how to get to heaven.

CHAPTER 5
IDENTITY CHANGE

If you have given your life to God, totally surrendered to Christ, then you are not that same old person who used to ... My physical body is 50 years old, but that's not the real me. I totally surrendered my life to Christ, and started growing in Him at the age of 23—that is, when my body was 23 and the old man that I used to be was 23. Now—as of then—I am a new creation, created in Christ, so I am 27 in truth. I must tell people that I am 50 because that is what they see, but I also say that even though I look older I feel like I'm 27. I don't identify with the old man anymore, now I identify with Christ and to all those around me I am Jesus—I'm His personal representative.

THE OLD MAN

Before I was born again, born a new person in Jesus, called to do as Jesus did, I was a sinner, and so were you. The word **sinner** means one who practices sin and does not receive Jesus as Lord, the One to obey. (This definition is not from the dictionary but from a Biblical view.) So, face it, before you accepted Jesus as Lord to obey Him you were a sinner. That might make some of you think. GOOD! I remember, many years ago in Massachusetts one time when my mom was drunk she confessed Jesus as Lord in front of me, just to get me off her back. She no more meant it than eggs are flat.

Have you confessed Jesus as Lord? Did you mean it in your heart? Are you continuing what Jesus had started (Acts 1:1) by doing what he did (John 14:12)? If you honestly answered yes to all three of these questions then I want you to look carefully at this verse.

"This means that anyone who belongs to Christ has become a new person. The old life is gone; a new life has begun!" (2 Corinthians 5:17 NLT).

That simply means that, although you may not look or sound or smell any different, inside is a newly created person with a new nature. Whereas, you used to have a nature of sin telling you to disobey your parents and do what is unhealthy, immoral, fattening, corrupt and just plain wrong; you now have exchanged that old nature for the nature of Jesus that wants to please His Father who is also your Father.

I once saw a good friend of mine with a shirt that read, "I am a sinner." I wanted to jump all over him because he was a Holy Spirit baptized believer, and no sinner could be baptized in the Holy Spirit. But the verse, wrongly written, which he thought backed that statement is,

"Here is a trustworthy saying that deserves full acceptance: Christ Jesus came into the world to save sinners—of whom I am the worst," (1 Timothy 1:15 NIV).

That may be a trustworthy statement, but it is also a misprinted verse. Paul knew that once a man is a new creation in Christ he is no longer a sinner; he may be tempted to sin and might sin every once in a while, but he doesn't practice sin and he has made Jesus his Lord to obey Him. Paul wrote 2 Corinthians 5:17, possibly, before 1 Timothy 1:15; so, this is how the verse probably was written,

"Here is a trustworthy saying that deserves full acceptance: Christ Jesus came into the world to save sinners—of whom I **was** the worst," (1 Timothy 1:15 NIV) **with word in boldface is changed from (am)**.

My question for you is: Are you a sinner still or are you obeying Jesus?

BE HIM

In the book of Acts Paul says that the disciples were called Christians, first at Antioch. Jesus said that those who believed in Him would do what He did, John 14:12. Then in Mark 16 He told of a few things that He did, "And these attesting signs will accompany those who believe," (Mark 16:17a).

"But you shall receive power (ability, efficiency, and might) when the Holy Spirit has come upon you, and you shall be My witnesses in Jerusalem and all Judea and Samaria and to the ends (the very bounds) of the earth," (Acts 1:8 AMP).

A witness tells of what he or she has heard and seen; Jesus is looking for you to be more than his witnesses, He wants you to be His representatives. Ya see, a representative does what the one he is representing does.

The president of America is supposed to be the leader of America, and the American ambassador is supposed to be the representative of the president to a foreign country. So, when the ambassador does something it is going to reflect on the reputation of the president. If the ambassador acts rudely in an official function it puts a bad light on the president and, subsequently, on America.

Look at an illustration:

The ambassador of America goes to an official treaty signing in Russia and gets drunk and cusses out a wife of a top Russian official. The president of the U.S. hears about it through a direct call from the Russian king; so he sends other representatives to try and make amends for the grief that the ambassador started. They even approach the ambassador about the wrong and he doesn't even recognize that he did anything wrong. What will happen if the ambassador is allowed to keep his position and never repents and apologizes to that guy and his wife?

Look at another illustration:

EMTs are representatives of a certain hospital, they're first responders and they come with the ambulance. A lady falls down her stairs and she has a deep gash on her thigh, it's bleeding profusely, it cut an artery. The ambulance comes and the EMTs put her on a stretcher and bring her in; but they did nothing but put a cause bandage on the gash. When they get to the hospital she is almost dead from bleeding. The head doctor in the E.R, approaches the EMTs and asks them why they didn't do anything about the deep arterial gash. They say, "We thought you would take care of that so we bandaged it." What do you think the doctor will do to them?

Brothers and sisters, you call yourselves Christians (representatives of the Christ). Are you doing what a true representative should do or do you want to be fired? Yes, Jesus went and talked to people of all characters, whores, tax collectors, Pharisees, Sadducees (sad people) … He confronted religious heresy. But He was sent to Earth to right wrongs—to make a few changes back to the way God intended them to be in the first place. How did He do that? Jesus laid hands on the sick, Jesus cast out demons, Jesus spoke things that didn't appear as though they were, Jesus spoke in tongues … What else did He do? He didn't tell His disciples to do anything that He didn't do Himself.

I'm not telling you that you must make the opportunity to cast out a demon and then cast it out in Jesus' name and I'm not telling you that if there is no need apparent to lay hands you the sick you must make the opportunity. But, if the need is there and the opportunity is presented to you and you slough it off thinking that only Jesus can heal them because, "After all, He is God and I am not." If you are a representative of Him and you're not doing what a representative should do then what Mr. 'T' used to say fits. "I pity the fool," don't be that fool, do what Jesus did.

The ambassador of America is the main representative of our president, he is our president to the foreign countries that he is sent to. Jesus was God's ambassador to the Earth. The EMTs are the representatives of the hospital that sent them, to the patient they are supposed to be the hospital (so-to-speak). You are a representative of Jesus the Christ, you should be Jesus to those whom you are sent to. Are you? You still have time.

The rapture is coming soon, I don't know the day or hour, all I know is that the season is rapidly approaching, I can read the signs of the times. When Jesus comes to get His own ... His own what? I believe it is His own true representatives that He is coming for; then the rest of you have seven more years, hard years, but if you're not ready by then it's too late.

ACTS

In the book of Acts, Jesus was talking to his disciples—those who had *already* confessed that He is Lord. He was talking to believers when He said this.

"But you will receive power when the Holy Spirit has come on you, and you will be My witnesses in Jerusalem, in all Judea and Samaria, and to the ends of the earth." (Acts 1:8 HCSB).

"But you shall receive power (ability, efficiency, and might) when the Holy Spirit has come upon you, and you shall be My witnesses in Jerusalem and all Judea and Samaria and to the ends (the very bounds) of the earth." (Acts 1:8 AMP).

The word **witnesses** does give the impression that all you need to do is talk about what Jesus did; but, what about the power that you will receive when the Holy Spirit has come *upon* you? According to the Amplified Bible this power is ability (words not written there are (**to do** something). According to *Steadfast in Honor* Acts 1:6-8 say,

"The followers asked Joshua, 'Are You going to establish Your kingdom here on Earth now?'

"To this He answered, 'No worries. That time is not now and you don't need to know when it will be. Just know this, you shall be enveloped in power once you are baptized in the Holy Spirit. This must be by your acceptance because the Father will never force anything upon anyone. But when you have this power you will witness—represent and spread the good news—of me, starting at home then spreading out,'" (Acts 1:6-8 SIH).

The word **represent** gives the meaning of doing the same as. A representative is, more than likely, someone who is totally committed to the one he is representing, in many cases this takes time. My son would represent me at a business meeting, he would go in my stead, take my authority; but, would he stop at that? What if there was something there that needed my signature. He has the authority to sign it for me. What if a need was present to fix a slide projector—and he knew how to do that because I had taught him—and they needed me to fix it. The boy is my representative, the boy is me

66

to them, he would fix it. My representative can and does do what I do, as long as he knows what I do; I work through my representative. Jesus represented God on earth, He was anointed (baptized) in God (the Holy Spirit), He did what God did.

The Gospels are full of what Jesus did and what he wants to do through His representatives—us. And if you are baptized in the Holy Spirit then the Holy Spirit has come upon you and you have received the power to do what Jesus did—He can work through you.

Now, in America we have a saying, "I dare you." Some people pass up the dare because it is stupid, depending upon what the dare is. I think it is Texas where this saying came from, "I double-dog dare you." That's a challenge and kids think '*Well, I can't let that one slide. I have to do it now, he double-dog dared me,*' but then most adults would still not go for it, depending upon what it is. What do you think, is there some truth to that?

Well, you say that you are a Christian and you have been filled with the Holy Spirit. Well, according to Acts 1:8 you can do the things that Jesus said to do in Mark 16:17-18. So, if that's the case then I double-dog (Texas) dare you to be a representative of Jesus. There are initials that God gave me, to make it humorous. D.E.D.T.A.C. (Dare Every Day To Act Christ) this is, in essence what Christian means.

D.E.T.A.C.H. means Dare Eternally To Acts like a Christian Hero. Romans 12:1-2 tell you to

D.E.T.A.C.H. from the world system and I double-dog (Texas) dare you to D.E.D.T.A.C.

NEW IDENTITY

When you first accepted and confessed Jesus as Lord, when you did that in all honesty and wanted what you were saying, this is what the Bible say happened,

"The angel replied, "The Holy Spirit will come upon you, and the power of the Most High will overshadow you. So the baby to be born will be holy, and he will be called the Son of God," (Luke 1:35 NLT).

The power of the Most High is the Holy Spirit, and He will overshadow or come over you. Many people seem to think that the Holy Spirit comes in you, but this verse doesn't say that, indeed, no verses say that. And it says that the baby will be holy, the Son of God. I believe that this happens to every person who accepts Jesus as Lord by a faith filled confession. And, it also doesn't say that the Holy Spirit stays, does it?

The Holy Spirit (the power of God) made love to Mary and inseminated her with fertile seed; He planted in her the seed to the fruit of the Spirit, that fruit was and is

68

Jesus. Jesus is (pardon the pun) the true Love Child, His Father is Love and He is Love.

EIGHT ASPECTS OF THE FRUIT

As has been established, Jesus is the fruit of the Spirit and He is love (you could capitalize it if you want).

"But the fruit of the [Holy] Spirit [the work which His presence within accomplishes] is love, joy (gladness), peace, patience (an even temper, forbearance), kindness, goodness (benevolence), faithfulness, Gentleness (meekness, humility), self-control (self-restraint, continence). Against such things there is no law [that can bring a charge]," (Galatians 5:22-23 AMP).

The Amplified Bible says, "[the work which His presence within accomplishes],' but according to Luke 1:35 that is not what it should say; it should say, "[the aspects of Jesus]."

If the fruit of the Spirit is love, then what about joy, peace, patience, kindness, goodness, faithfulness, gentleness and self-control; are they fruit? These are aspects of love; to be more specific, these are category names of the fruit, which is love (Jesus). Isn't or couldn't love be an aspect of the fruit of the Spirit? Yes, that is a possible thought, but for now we will look at the other eight aspects. You will notice that the Amplified Bible gives only a few synonyms of some of these aspects, but there are many more. For instance faithfulness includes being trustworthy, true, and loyal; patience includes being steadfast (always being the same), constant, calm, and temperate; and joy includes being in calm delight, and jubilant.

Okay, you twisted my arm, I will share a bit about love as a *category title* of aspects of Love (the characteristics of the nature of Jesus).

CHAPTER 6
THE CATEGORY OF LOVE

The first aspect in this category of the fruit of the Spirit (the characteristic of the nature of Jesus) is forgiveness.

FORGIVENESS

Example #1

I want to share something with you about forgiveness that happened to my friend Jake. At one point Jake was in surgery to have his colon removed because it was about as useful as a dead ant to him. Anyway, when the surgeon removed it he said that in a short time he could do the corrective surgery. The specialist told Jake that his surgeon had removed the muscle that was needed before the corrective surgery could be done. Jake's surgeon did not tell him that; in fact, he told him everything was fine. He lied to Jake in an area that, to him, was an almost life or death matter. Don't you know that that really hurt my friend? But what could Jake do now? After a while he realized that he had to forgive the doctor, so he did and then prayed for a new muscle. It wasn't long after that that he had that new muscle. Also during that original surgery Jake had major complications.

He had to have a double operation that took ten hours and resulted in a total mess. As a result of this another organ in his body was ruined, which could have been avoidable if the second surgeon would have listened to God. But Jake forgave him too and God gave him a promise, God is good for His Word.

Example #2

Another situation that my friend at church told me happened in his life, he and his wife. The man's wife was raped. She was a true Christian and knew the commandment of love, of which forgiveness is a part. The two were faced with a choice, to either forgive that rapist or hold a grudge. That was a very hard decision to make, they laid awake nights thinking about that incident. It was causing them real anguish, the husband was getting sick and he even lost time at work. Finally, he came to Christ and they both forgave the rapist, not face to face but in their prayer time, then he started feeling better and was being more successful at his job and going forward in life.

What would you do if someone hurt you like they did these two people? Turn, if you would, to Matthew 18:21 and read the whole parable with your friends. Then look at verse 35, it says,

"This is how my heavenly Father will treat each of you unless you forgive your brother or sister from your heart," (Matthew 18:35 NIV).

If you don't forgive someone who wrongs you in any way what do you think or how should you expect God to act on your behalf?

Example #3

As you can probably see, there are great benefits to forgiving others no matter how tough the situation might be, no matter what they did to you. I just started reading a book about a band; they were all seniors in high school. One of the guys in the band, William, was punched in the nose by the school bully and knocked off his feet. A friend of William's who was on the wrestling team attacked the bully to keep him from hurting William any more. Then William got up and told the wrestler to stop, and told all who were present that he forgave the bully and he loved him. As a result both the wrestler and the bully got born again. Many things have totally turned from bad to good because of forgiveness. So then, knowing that God wants to forgive you, you can walk in forgiveness and expect Him to forgive you. Then you can say 'T.G.I.F. (Thank God I'm Forgiven).'

FORGIVE

And, on the flip side of being forgiven, we should respond by forgiving others. There are many ways that people, these days, use to convey forgiveness. How did Jesus do this or how did He say to do it?

When you say or do something that hurts someone else, maybe you said something that hurt his or her feelings, you should apologize. "But I didn't intend to hurt them, they just took it that way," you might say. Well, maybe you didn't but that person was hurt anyway. One time I invited my neighbor to a meeting and the preacher asked if anyone wanted to receive the Holy Spirit, as you know there are denominations that believe that when you get born again you are automatically baptized with the Holy Spirit but that's not true. I asked my neighbor if she wanted to receive this gift and she took it as if I were accusing her of not being born again. I had to apologize.

Anyway, when you apologize, the best way to do that is by saying, "I'm sorry for ...," and meaning it You have just released yourself from guilt. But now it's their turn, they must forgive you or they will begin to get bitter and feel guilty. Now, how is this too be done? The best way to forgive is, well of course it's got to be from the heart, from the heart and with the words "I forgive you." Not by simple saying, "Forget it," and not by saying, "It's alright." Saying, "It's alright," makes it sound like what the person did wasn't wrong and he or she can go ahead and do it again. "Take heed to yourselves. If your brother
74

sins against you, rebuke him; and if he repents, forgive him." (Luke 17:3 NKJV)

I want to tell you a story: One day Sam, who was a Spirit filled Christian, did something against God. It was purely unintentional but John saw it and rebuked Sam. Then John prayed for Sam and asked God to forgive him. Sam went to God and repented and God said, "It's alright." Sam said, "But I thought it was a sin so I'm repenting." Then God said, "Forget it." Then Sam went to John and said, "I repented but I don't think God is willing to forgive me."

Why did Sam get the idea that God wouldn't forgive him? Maybe it's because God didn't use the words "I forgive you."

Now, take a look at these verses:

"Then Peter came to Jesus and asked, 'Lord, when my fellow believer sins against me, how many times must I forgive him? Should I forgive him as many as seven times?' Jesus answered, 'I tell you, you must forgive him more than seven times. You must forgive him even if he wrongs you seventy times seven," (Matthew 18:21-22 NCV).

In other words, as many times as needed. Seventy times seven is 490 times; you can't do that in one day, no one can sin against you that much in one day.

What if Peter came to Jesus and said, "Lord, this guy sinned against me and I forgave him, I said, 'It's alright,' but he did it again and again. Each time he did it to me I told him I didn't like it, and he apologized so I said, 'Forget it, just don't do it again.' Later on he did it again, it's getting on my nerves and I don't like it. What should I do?"

"Forgive him," Jesus said.

"But I did, and he keeps doing it as if it was alright."

"That's because you said it was alright," Jesus explained. "Instead, Why don't you use the words, 'I forgive.' He'll get the message soon enough. And keep using those words and do it from your heart until He stops doing it."

"I forgive, huh, I never thought about that."

Well, that's the trouble, people don't think of that. And do you know why? Because it's too easy. Many people seem to think that the Christian life has to be hard, that they either have to try, on their own, to figure out words to use in place of the words used in the Bible or they can only use the words that a preacher taught them, a preacher who might have gotten bad teaching. Or they might think that the Bible can only be interpreted by the Pope, but they never listen to the Pope. And why does the Pope have exclusive rights to the interpreting of the Bible that was authored by God?

When someone does you wrong use the words, 'I forgive you,' when forgiving them. You'd be surprised at the outcome.

GIVING AND RECEIVING

Another area of love that we, as Christians, can and should be practicing is the area of giving (God is a benevolent God). Remember that "God so loved the world that HE GAVE ..." (John 3:16a). That is one thing that we as Christians are not doing enough of, and I'm not just talking about money. You know, Christians should be known as givers among people. Christians have so much to give, or at least they should have, and I'm not talking about just spiritual words or money. I'm talking about wisdom, encouragement, love, comfort, help, shelter ... (the list goes on). However, the ministry of spreading God's Word needs money just like businesses, to operate.

There is a principle that's called the hundred-fold principle or the seed-plant harvest principle. What God said in it is that when you give, depending upon your faith, you can receive a hundred-fold in return. Of course, you must not give grudgingly or because your pastor told you that 'If you don't give $...... we're going down the drain.' For God loves, *He loves*, a cheerful giver. Now, don't give with the wrong motives, such as giving to get or to out give someone else (so as to say 'Look, God, I'm a big giver.'), give out of a loving heart. But when you give be ready to receive.

Look at Proverbs 19:17 with me, here Solomon said "He who is kind to the poor lends to the Lord, and he (the Lord) will reward him for what he has done," (NIV) the New King James Version says "has pity on." To have pity on is to show love toward. There are people out there who give to the poor just because they see the need. There are people who actually dig down to the last penny in their savings accounts just because they see someone in more need than they. I also know of church bodies that raise money to feed the dirtiest, ugliest person in town. I also know of people who support these ministries financially that want, are heart hungry, to spread God's love in any and every way possible. I know some people personally who are on Social Security, making $50 above rent and bills and use that $50 to support the ministry. And I also know of people, whether they be monetarily rich or not, who sit on what they have and make a quest to get more.

The givers, those who give cheerfully, are the happy people. In 2 Corinthians 9:6 Paul said that the one who gives generously will reap generously. Then in verse 7 he said, "*So let* each one *give* as he purposes in his heart, not grudgingly or of necessity; for God loves a cheerful giver." (NKJV) This leads me to think that the amount that I have decided to give, after talking to God about it, is a generous amount. This is always a good amount because I can give it joyfully, and that's what God loves.

God is not as interested in your giving as He is in your willingness to give, your cheerful attitude. If you can't give cheerfully He would rather you not give at all, He doesn't appreciate your giving with a stingy attitude. But if you have a cheerful attitude about giving and you do have something to give then I've got one word for you; GIVE. Something to give does not always have to mean money.

"[Remember] this: he who sows sparingly and grudgingly will also reap sparingly and grudgingly, and he who sows generously and that blessings will come to someone, will also reap generously and with blessings. Let each one give as he has made up in his own mind and purposed in heart, not reluctantly or sorrowfully or under compulsion, for God loves (that is, he takes pleasure in, prizes above other things, and is unwilling to abandon or to do without) a cheerful (joyous, prompt-to-do-it) giver-whose heart is in his giving," (2 Corinthians 9:6-7 AMP).

Now, if you will, look with me at Proverbs 22:9, "Blessed are those who are generous, because they feed the poor." (NLT) In the Greek, The word 'blessed' means 'happy.' That is why I say that those who have learned the art of giving are the happy people.

Another thing is; if those poor people, talked about in a previous paragraph, will receive it, God won't have them stay poor for long. I know because I was one of those poor people, sickness had taken all of my money away, but even though I had no money I kept giving, I gave of what I had. The generosity that God taught me kept the poverty that Satan threw at me from making me sink.

COMPASSION

What is compassion? Well, some say it is love, as in love for all. And, I guess you could take that view and not be out of bounds. The Webster's dictionary says it is sorrow or pity, sympathy. I hope you don't take that view because it is not sympathy, that is a worldly feeling of what they call compassion. Although there is an inkling of pity in compassion it is not sorrow at all, it's reaching out to do something. As you read the Bible and talk to your loving God you will realize that compassion is a deep desire, from deep within the bowels of your being, to act in merciful love, it's a need to help someone in need.

Let's look at a verse of the Bible about compassion and see what we can see.

"But when he saw the multitudes, he was moved with compassion on them, because they fainted, and were scattered abroad, as sheep having no shepherd," (Matthew 9:36 NKJV).

When Jesus saw the crowd He was *moved* with compassion, that tells me that compassion, while it is love toward all, is a force.

When Jesus was moved with compassion He was moved into action, now let's see what He did.

"And when Jesus went out He saw a great multitude; and He was moved with compassion for them, and healed their sick, (Matthew 14:14 NKJV).

Other verses, such as Matthew 18:27, say that when other people were moved with compassion they did things like forgive great debts.

We can pray for ourselves, and we can be moved with compassion and pray for others. When Jesus prayed for others He already knew God's Will on the subject so He just prayed the prayer of thanksgiving, thanked God for the answer that He promised. Jesus never had to plead with God for someone's healing or for someone's (something else that was in God's Will). And if it wasn't God's Will He just would not pray for it, He wasn't going to go against God's Will.

When someone comes to you with a need for prayer, do you pray for him or her as if you were praying for yourself? I guarantee you that if you did you would be more earnest about seeing the results. Compassion in prayer, then, is putting yourself in the place of that person whom you are praying for. "Bear one another's burdens, and so fulfill the law of Christ, (Galatians 6:2 NKJV). This is not talking about taking worry and all that junk and keeping it. No, it's simply telling us to help them as if the problems are our own. Now, if you had a sickness or a grief or whatever wouldn't you want to get rid of it as soon as you could and go on living the worry free life that God intended for you?

I had a friend from Oral Roberts University who was looking for a job, he didn't have a car so I drove him to some places to apply. When I brought him back to his dorm he asked me to pray with him for some money to do his laundry. This is where compassion moved me to share. As I was praying God reminded me that I had some money in my wallet so I shared with him because if you can move to meet the need, God called us to be need meeters. I believed God for a financial breakthrough myself. "For as the body without the spirit is dead, so faith without works is dead also, (James 2:26 NKJV). I had what he needed and God had what I needed. It's a spiritual law set down by God Himself that if I give to meet someone's need the (G)god of that someone will give to meet my need (Philippians 4:15-19).

So, when someone comes to you for prayer, whether it is in a prayer line at church or not, see that person as yourself and their need as your need. If you do you will have a deeper desire to see that need met, you won't just pray a lesc-fair prayer and forget it, you're going to see it through to the desired result. If it's healing you are going to, first see yourself with that need and then pray, thank God, for healing then call yourself and the other person healed.

I know this is hard to do, but what you should be doing is imitating Jesus and what he did. You are being a little Jesus to that person, as a substitute.

CHAPTER 7
THE CATEGORY OF JOY

If a person is walking in true love and representing Jesus the Christ as being alive today that person will know joy and its inclusions.

SYNONYMS

Let me give you some synonyms of joy. We have jubilance (and there we go with dancing, clapping, singing, and the like), enchantment (as in "Have an enchanted time"). Then I found a word that will knock your socks off, the word rapture. When you think of the rapture a great joy should overwhelm you, at least it does me. The next word is delight (as in "Delight yourself in the Lord.").

STRENGTH

Joy is a major attribute of the fruit of the Spirit; this is because if you don't know joy, the joy of the Lord, you can't really be strong. Until you are born again (born of the Spirit of God) you can't really know this joy. You might be experiencing happiness and think it's joy but it's not. Joy is an amazing spiritual force. I say this because without joy you would find it very difficult to operate in the fruit of the Spirit. Indeed, later in this book you will find out that it is impossible.

His joy is my strength. Did you get that? The joy of the Lord is my strength. You see, the joy of the Lord and strength are synonymous terms. "Although you may seem strong in the natural, I tell you the truth, until you are born again and filled with joy you aren't really strong," so says the Lord. I urge you to ask Him yourself.

GIVING

If you are a born again Christian and you say that you have not much joy, you need to get into giving. This I found through experience, and the Bible speaks of it too; giving increases joy!!! I was ministering to a young woman a while ago about joy. Then I said, "If this doesn't help you I will come down there and give you my joy because it can't do anything but give me more." Actually, I can't give you my joy, but I can minister joy to you and your joy will rise up within you. A Scripture to back this up is,

"Go and enjoy choice food and sweet drinks, and send some to those who have nothing prepared. This day is sacred to our Lord. Do not grieve, for the joy of the LORD is your strength," (Nehemiah 8:10 NIV).

Every time I give money, I give not just from my wallet but also from my heart and the giving always gives me joy unspeakable. The first thing that you must do, though, in your giving is you must first give yourself to the Lord. If you don't give yourself to the Lord first your financial giving, plus everything else, may help others, but it will profit the giver (you) nothing.

IN HIS PRESENCE

Psalm 16:11 tells us that in the presence of the Lord there is fullness of joy. In the presence of the Lord there's joy, do you realize what that means? You cannot go before the Lord and remain grumpy or sorrowful, it's impossible. This joy will just rise up within you.

For example, suppose I was feeling pretty grumpy and sorrowful, carrying the cares of whatever. When I go to the Lord, and do what His Word says and cast my cares upon the Lord, I can't stay feeling grumpy or sorrowful anymore. There's nothing about God to feel grumpy or sorrowful about. Now, don't get this confused with *looking* upset, I'll tell you what I mean. A while ago I was upset about a letter ministry that I was performing. I went to the Lord about it, afterwards I was looking upset (I was still crying a little) but I wasn't grumpy and I wasn't really sorrowful (only by appearance). This is because there was now a calmness (an unexplainable peace) within me. What was happening was I was taking the cares of the ministry (God's ministry) upon myself, He gave me encouragement.

We read a bit about joy in the book of Isaiah, Isaiah 65:14. It tells us that the Lord's sons (born again Christians) should be joyful, but the wicked shall be sorrowful. Ya see, this joy is in the heart of man, the core, in his spirit.

Did you know that the unbeliever can have joy? But it only lasts for a moment then it's gone. Like when a man living by faith and confessing his faith in healing has to go to the hospital, the wicked find joy in that, but it doesn't last. So, joy for the unbeliever is just for a moment, that's the world's version of joy. But joy stays with the Holy Spirit of God.

We see, in God's Word, that faith comes when you hear the Word of God. Well, so does joy. We find out from John 16:22 that joy comes to our hearts (spirits) when we seek the Lord. To tell you the truth, joy is in us already simply because we are born again. But when we seek audience with the Lord, as the Scripture said, there's joy in His presence. I'll tell you a few more ways that you can call upon the joy that the Holy Spirit planted in your spirit. When you pray, we found, is one way. When you dwell on the Word of God, simply reading it or hearing it, is another because God's promises are facts in themselves. Also, taking the Word of God and whipping the devil up side the head with it and putting him where he belongs is another way to call on joy. Another way is to act upon your commitment of love and to walk the love walk, even in the face of your enemies. In fact, everything positive said about loving God, the how-to's, is calling upon the joy of the Lord. Then in John 16:24 we find that one of the ways it increases is by receiving from God.

1 Peter 1:4 tells us that we who love the Lord do so without seeing Him, His joy overflows in our hearts and this is all by faith, and because of all this we are full of glory. I'm hearing people say, "But I didn't think we were supposed to get any glory." Jesus said in prayer to the Father, "And the glory which You gave Me I have given them (talking about us), that they may be one just as We are one," (John 17:22 NKJV). Only by the Holy Spirit can you operate in this kind of love, and it is by your will that you believe, and there's joy in believing. Remember, happiness is not joy, not this kind of joy.

Happiness is an offspring of joy but when I said happiness is not joy ... well, let me explain in more detail. The world equates happiness and joy as 'kissing cousins' or the same, most equate them as the same, but there is a vast difference between true happiness and true joy. True happiness in the Greek means being blessed. That has to do with a lot of things; confession of the tongue is one. Proverbs 18:21a tells us that death (and the curse) and life (and the blessings) are in the power of the tongue. This means that you can speak blessings upon yourself over and over and soon they will take a hold in your life. Or you can do the opposite and speak cursing upon yourself. I said happiness is the offspring of joy only because in order to start this inflow of happiness you must first get born again. Jesus tells us, in the book of John that for the mere fact that the Word is in you; you are filled with joy. However, when you are blessed and happy, joy will rise up to the surface many times to the point of overflowing.

Worldly happiness is not being blessed; all it is is a false feeling brought on by having plenty of money, having a beautiful woman love you, or whatever.

When this true happiness and true joy rise up some people get fearful, they don't want to be around you or talk to you because they feel a conviction or uneasiness when they are around you. This has happened to me on many occasions. Sometimes it will so overwhelm you that you will get loud.

CHEERFULNESS

Let me tell you a true story about me a long time ago. I was nearly broke, I had four quarters in my pocket and a little money set aside for bills sitting in my dresser at home. Yes, I had already given my tithe. I was sitting in church and the offering plate came my way so, out of a sense of obligation, I reached in my pocket for the quarters to put them in the plate. Just then God spoke up and said to me, "Don't put them in."

I went out into the hall and asked God why, "Why shouldn't I give the money?"

He said, "Because your heart isn't in it. I would rather you not give your money and have a good attitude than to give your money with a rotten attitude." See, it's the good attitude that accompanies the giving that He can bless-add on to not the money. Oh, He may use money to do it but He cannot bless a rotten attitude. He was teaching me something by this, and you will notice that He didn't just let me give with that bad attitude and then tell me what I did wrong.

"Let each one [give] as he has made up his own mind and purposed in his heart, not reluctantly or sorrowfully or under compulsion, for God loves (He takes pleasure in, prizes above other things, and is unwilling to abandon or to do without) a cheerful (joyous, "prompt to do it") giver [whose heart is in his giving]," (2 Corinthians 9:7 AMP).

    The lesson that God was teaching me is taken from this verse; many preachers have preached this verse while giving their tithes and offerings message but neglected to expound on it. So let me take this verse (you can look at verses 1-13 later but look here now). "Let each one [give] as he has made up his own mind and purposed in his *heart*," my heart is filled with the love of God, in other words God fills my heart. That means that if I am going to give as I purpose in my heart—in my God-filled heart—then I am going to ask my God to direct my giving. Then, and only then, (after I have purposed in my heart) will my mind be made up. *"Not reluctantly or sorrowfully or under compulsion,"* if you are listening to God then you won't be listening to any compelling argument from any preacher and you won't be reluctant or sorrowful in your giving either. "For God loves (He takes pleasure in, prizes above other things, and is unwilling to abandon or to do without) a cheerful (joyous, "prompt to do it") giver [whose heart is in his giving]." Now, if you are in God and He is in you, both intertwined, (John 15:7) then by letting God direct your giving you are doing it out of and in love. Your attitude will be one of joy and you will be prompt to give with peace, and that is when your heart will be in your giving. (By the way; if you have $1000 neither $10 nor $1000 is giving abundantly if you are not giving from the heart).

So, this is all about listening to God. The difference about the tithe is that the tithe is a set amount. Yes it varies with your income, sure, it is a percentage, **tithe** means tenth, it also means the first fruits. If your total income form week one is $234 then the tithe is the first $23.40, anything above it is an additional offering; and anything below that is an offering too. If for week two it is $229.45 then your tithe is $22.94 (why not round that off to $22.95). Some said that giving the tithe is mandatory but it is not really, but there are great benefits for tithing. In other words, if you have not given your tithe first then giving an offering doesn't really do much for the giver. Also, when you are committed to giving the tithe (or tithing) it builds your character and you have more probability for increase in your life. I have heard people say that they gave their tithe (which, by the way, was only 7% of their income) to so-n-so (an evangelistic ministry in another state).

"Bring all the tithes into the storehouse so there will be enough food in my Temple. If you do," says the LORD of Heaven's Armies, "I will open the windows of heaven for you. I will pour out a blessing so great you won't have enough room to take it in! Try it! Put me to the test!" (Malachi 3:10 NLT).

They didn't tithe, did they? First of all, they only sent 7% (the tithe is the first 10%) and, secondly, they sent it to another place, not the storehouse, which is their local church where they are (hopefully) members.

Let me reverse this verse to show you what will not happen if you don't do it. "*Don't* bring all the tithes into the storehouse (sent it off somewhere else) so there will *not* be enough food in my Temple. If you do*n't*," says the LORD of Heaven's Armies, "I will *not* open the windows of heaven for you. I will *not* pour out a blessing so great you won't have enough room to take it in! Try it! Put me to the test!"

It's like this, the tithe is the cake and the offerings is the icing (bad grammar, I know). A misplaced cake gets no icing. And who puts icing on a cake that's partially there, not whole? You can't put icing on a cake that's not been baked either.

Giving the tithe is giving, but the tithe is a set percentage of your income, it's not 9% or less and it's not 11% or more. I've heard some people say, "I'm going to start tithing 20%." Well, they're either lying or they are just using the wrong words, because the tithe is 10%, the first 10%. What they, probably, mean is that they are going to give the first 20% of their income, make it a true first fruit double.

So anyway, I did go to church that evening and I gave those four quarters with joy because I had talked to God about it. Sometimes what the preacher would do, but God won't (not normally), is have you give all you have, "because it's a worthy cause." Yes, the most worthy cause is God but if He doesn't teach His people to save money His kingdom would come into bankruptcy and He doesn't want that. It would because not all of God's children know how to manage money correctly.

Yes, not tithing is robbing God, but also withholding both your tithes *and* your offerings is robbing God (Malachi 3:3). So, while tithing is, indeed, optional, it is also advisable, so is giving offerings. Another difference is that while the tithe goes to the storehouse and it's set at 10%, offerings can go anywhere and they are not a certain percent. None of this can be done without joy, joy is the release for your giving.

CHAPTER 8
CATEGORY OF PEACE

If a person is walking in true love and representing Jesus the Christ as being alive today that person will have the peace of God. Get to know peace and its inclusions.

SYNONYMS

Some synonyms for peace are serenity, rest, harmony, and tranquility, and security. I'm sure you know of the Serenity Prayer, you probably thought of that as soon as I mentioned serenity. Well, now that we found out that God has planted in us the seed of serenity and we have the mind of Christ (1 Corinthians 2:16), the wisdom and knowledge of God, I guess saying that prayer as a request doesn't make much sense. I looked up some synonyms of security from above and found assurance, guarantee, insurance, certainty, and (this is an interesting one) promise, which means to warrant or assure. This kind of peace is inner peace, as we will soon find out. This is the peace that gives you certainty that the Word of God is true. It will also help you to stay calm while people all around you are at war with one another; while everything gets disturbed you won't. Many of you have heard the term 'Blessed Assurance', it's also the title of a song, well that's peace. This peace is, to use a stronger word, our guarantee that what God promised He would do for you He'll do.

INNER AND OUTER PEACE

My heart and soul are at peace on a day to day basis. I have, taped to my Bible, a commitment prayer which I speak over myself daily telling God of my commitment to Him, also telling myself what I am to be doing. Then I make it a point to spend a while reading His Word and praying before I do any work. (This is what I do; you might do something else. If what you're doing is alright with God then you don't have to change.) I do this and am certain that I have the peace of God during the day. At night I thank God for the peace He has given me, which I have with Him. I do everything I know to do to have peace with God because when I am at peace with God I have His protection. Let me give you an example: When the Gibeonites made a peace treaty with the Israelites (Joshua chapter 9) the Israelites had to protect them. The original plan that God had for Israel was that they destroy the Gibeonites along with the rest. But since the treaty was made God told Israel that they had to protect the Gibeonites, even though the treaty was made under deception (Gibeon deceived Israel).

Peace is, again, a major attribute of the fruit of the Spirit. Without peace you would have an impossible time operating in joy. Remember, one of the meanings of joy is calm delight (peaceful delight). There's peace in believing, that is believing the Word of God.

"May the God of your hope so fill you with all joy and peace in believing-through the experience of your faith-that by the power of the Holy Spirit you may abound and be overflowing (bubbling over) with hope," (Romans 15:13 AMP).

To have faith in God is to trust, receive from, and obey Him, and that is one effect of love. We see here that faith, hope, peace and joy work together. So now, what does that tell you about love, those four and love?

I'm sure you know that you can have peace in the midst of war, it's inner peace. War and inner turmoil are two different things. Inner peace and inner turmoil are opposites just as outer peace and war are opposites. But you cannot have this peace if you are in fear; fear is inner turmoil. When a person is in fear he worries, which is anxiety. And anxiety is opposed to peace, talking about inner peace.

"Casting (cast) the whole of your care-all your anxieties, all your worries, all your concerns, once and for all-on Him: for He cares for you affectionately, cares about you watchfully," (1 Peter 5:7 AMP).

"Let Him have all your worries and cares, for He is always thinking about you and watching everything that concerns you," (same verse NLT).

By doing this you can maintain, or keep, yourself in the peace of God. Isn't that a thrill? He will swap His peace for your anxieties, just like He swapped His Son's right standing for our sins, when Jesus became sin for us. Of course, Jesus didn't stay a sinner but we are still righteous, we who have confessed to receive Jesus as Lord.

SLEEP

John 14:27 tells us that the Lord will give us peace. The Lord had said this to us, He gave it to us, now it's up to us to live in it. Have you ever had those nights when you just couldn't sleep straight through the night, and when you got up you were still tired? If you are like I was those nights are practically every night. Psalm 4:8 gives us an 'out' in that area. It says that it is entirely possible for me and you to sleep calmly all night, not to wake up at all hours of the night, and be totally rested in the morning. It says I go to sleep in peace because it is my Lord who makes me dwell in safety (or dwell securely). There is peace in my heart when I go to bed because I am safe and in right standing with the Lord. I sleep all night and am refreshed in the morning. You can have this peace too if you are in right standing with God.

As I said, the Lord has made a way that I can sleep calmly all night and wake up refreshed in the morning because I have peace with God. But occasionally I would have a restless night. I asked the Lord why this was and He told me that I was taking the cares of my (whatever) upon myself. He said, "I told you to cast all your cares on me." That goes in any area of life. You cannot remain at peace if you are carrying the cares of ... anything. Anyway, when I do that I go to bed and sleep calmly.

Be smart enough to know that God knows the situation you're in and trust Him with it. If there is something you can't figure out go to the one who knows the answers.

Another thing that you must do is have faith in God. Trust in God, trust that He is always there for you if you believe in Him. God tells us, in the book of Isaiah, that the unbeliever has no peace. And we know why by simple definition, the unbeliever doesn't have peace because he has no faith in God. These people are restless inside. As I said in the chapter about commitment, people can try to fake most all of these attributes. Many times you will see an unbeliever who is very calm, cool, and collected. But if you could see their heart you would see the restlessness within.

Peace also comes by hearing the Word of God. In John 16:33a Jesus says "These things have I spoken unto you that in me you might have peace." (NKJV) Through the knowledge of Jesus Christ as Lord and knowing what His Word will do in us, for us, and through us peace will come. And you get that knowledge by reading the Word of God, and hearing it. When your thoughts are like Jesus' thoughts, that's peace.

AGREEMENT

"Can two walk together, except they be agreed?" (Amos 3:3 KJV) When someone agrees with you about something there is a peace between you two about that subject. Suppose you said, "I think the Toyota Camry is the best car around." But the guy you are talking with does not like the Toyota Camry. He will not agree with you, indeed there might be an argument about to arise. For whatever the reason, there is no peace going between you two about a Toyota Camry so there cannot be any agreement.

Now, you can drum up any subject you want to and I can guarantee that someone will argue with you. There are people out there who just want to argue, it makes them feel like they are so very important if they can win every argument. You must love them and try, probably with all you are, not to let them make you feel that you're stupid, you will loose your peace.

But anyway, when you find people who will agree with you, you have found people who are at peace with you. Usually this agreement, this peace, is found in people with certain similarities, such as clubs, fellowships, denominations, covens, churches, or parties. (I don't recommend covens).

A few pages ago I told you about the Gibeonites, how they deceived Israel and asked for a peace treaty. Non-Christians, even those who are Christian but have devils on their backs and don't care to get rid of them, will fix their eyes on you. They will use deception and give you the impression that they are right with God. Watch that you don't get deceived into making a peace treaty (contract, covenant, agreement) with them. You will be bound by your words.

CHAPTER 9
CATEGORY OF PATIENCE

Patience (longsuffering) is not only a vital part of the fruit of the Spirit but it is also something that everyone, whether born again or unbeliever, should know and use. I said it is a vital part because if you did not operate in patience you would not have peace, joy would not rise up, and patience is a direct attribute of love. Not only that, but nothing concerning the kingdom of God would work without patience. We'll see this as we go on in studying the fruit of the Spirit, also in studying the whole Bible, so keep patience in mind.

SYNONYMS

Here are some synonyms of patience, they are longanimous (charitable), longsuffering, and meek (not weak). Everywhere I go I hear people say "be patient." These people don't really know what they are saying. They should be saying, "don't rush the Lord," but they're actually saying, "wait and it will happen." Suppose we were dealing with the area of healing. The attitude I find in many people who say "be patient" is more of an attitude of '*Stop, don't believe the Lord for your healing anymore because after so long you should realize that maybe He's not going to give it to you.'* Or their attitude might be *'He'll give it to you when He is good and ready,'* or *'you never know what God's going to do.'* Folks, being patient does not mean laying down and waiting and letting Satan walk all over you. To be patient for my healing I've got to keep God's Word on healing going out of my mouth and into the ears of God, Satan, myself, and others, and I need to minister healing to others. Jeremiah 1:12 tells us that God confirms His Word, so does Mark 16:20, it's His Word that we speak. He'll only confirm it in our lives if we agree upon it and begin to confess it over ourselves.

You can see how vital patience is in the fruit of the Spirit because without patience there would be no calmness in the body and nothing involved would work. I have to stress that point so you will see the importance of patience. I can't rate the fruit of the Spirit from 1-9 because they are all attributes of love. But I'll just say this, without patience you might as well forget it.

PROTECTION

The opposite of patience is anxiety, don't let anxiety take rule in your life. Ya see, when you get anxious about something, 9 times out of 10, that anxiety will make you sick. The other one time would be because of a bad attitude or a lack of knowledge about what God said.

You have heard it many times and have probably read it in the Bible, "patiently wait." I tell you the truth, there is such a thing as anxiously waiting. This is waiting, but there is no calmness in the body. As I said, it could very possibly make you sick, maybe even go so far as to kill you, so the best way to stay away from that is by being patient.

When I drive down the road I try to go the speed limit. If there is someone behind me he either uses patience and stays calm or breaks the law by speeding past me, sometimes on a double solid line. That is what a lack of patience will do, it will always cause someone to break a law. Whether it is a spiritual law or a man made law it will always be broken by an impatient person. I give you a choice, only because the Lord gave it first, either use patient in all it's meanings or be a lawbreaker. I choose to operate in patience and be on the right side of the spiritual and man made laws.

The truth is, patience will keep you from going crazy. But, you need more than patience; you need patience plus love, joy, peace, plus all the rest that Gal. 5:22-23 talk about.

I'm sure you have heard it said, "be patient with one another," this is also written in the Bible. Well I would like to expound upon that phrase; be patient and wait on your brother and sister and don't count the seconds before they come through. If you wait with anxiety as your waiting partner where is your calmness (peace)? I tell you the truth, anxiety will drive you batty. So, be patient with your brother and sister as your heavenly Father is still being patient with you.

In Matthew chapter 18 Jesus tells a parable of a king who decided to have his accounting done and get his records straight with his subjects. There was one man who owed him quite a bit, we'll say $1,000,000,000.00, and he couldn't pay it back at that time. The king got a little mad and was about to sell all the man's property, including his wife and kids, so he could get his money. But the man begged the king to be patient with him. So the king, out of mercy and compassion, forgave the debt, cancelled it. Then that subject went out from the king's presence feeling good. He saw one of his brother subjects who owed him $10. The first guy grabbed his brother by the neck, started choking him, and demanded that he pay back that $10. That man begged him to be patient because he was very poor and didn't have any money. The first man would not be patient so he threw the second man in prison. Well, it wasn't long until the king heard about this, so he called for that first subject. He told him that he had pity on him when he asked for patience, and cancelled the debt. Then the king asked the man why, when the other guy asked him to be patient, he couldn't even be patient (bear with him)? Essentially, he was asking the man, "What happened to your joy, where did it go? Aren't you happy that you're free?" The king (the Lord) was patient with that man but that man had, evidently, a bad attitude about his brother. In one word I'll tell you what that man, evidently, lacked a realization of, LOVE.

Now, if I may I'd like to restate that parable, just to make it a little clearer. Suppose it was Pharaoh, and you were his servant back in the time of Moses. You owed Pharaoh, what's now equal to, $1,000,000,000.00. He called you in and demanded you pay him back, but you didn't have the money at the time, things were tough, there was a depression and a famine, and $1,000,000,000.00 back then was a lot of money. When he found out that you, a dumpy old servant, did not have the money to pay him back he was about to behead you. So, in desperation, you asked him, you begged him and pleaded with him, to be patient with you and you would repay all the debt. So he, being moved by compassion, forgave the debt completely. So, happily you went out and told your wife.

Later on you saw one of your friends who was also a servant of Pharaoh. This man owed you $5, so you grabbed him and started hurting him. "Pay back what you owe me!" you yelled at him. Another man who owed you $20, another one who owed $40, and still others who owed you different sums of money were there and you started yelling at all of them, you got very hot under the collar. You better watch out, all these guys might gang up on you. There was no forgiveness in your heart because you didn't know how to operate in patience, so you had them all thrown into jail. Pharaoh was told of your deeds and called you back in. He said, "I forgave you your big debt because you asked me to. Now, why couldn't you forgive a man a small debt? I should have just killed you as your deed deserved." Now, this Pharaoh represents God and you had that big debt called sin. He forgave you your sin, which deserved death. Now, why can't you

109

forgive someone a minor sin against you? If you don't forgive someone else when they sin against you, what do you think God should do? Believe it or not, that story of the king forgiving his servant began with patience. That, kind of, makes it sound like patience and forgiveness are tied in with each other, doesn't it?

"Be patient, therefore, brothers, until the coming of the Lord," (James 5:7a ESV). Our Lord has such great patience for us that after about 2000 He's still calmly waiting. We, some of us, have a hard time waiting 20 minutes. Now, why is that, or why should that be? Don't you think there should be a change in people, both non-Christians and Christians alike? If the Lord didn't have such great patience none of us would be saved, none of us would be going to heaven, for that matter none of us would even be alive now. If He can be so patient, Christians, shouldn't it stand that we should be a 'patient bread' also? I mean, to you who are born again, He's in us and if He's in us then His patience is in us to use.

STEADFASTNESS

Ya know, Abraham was promised that he and his wife would have a son—not by adoption—even though Abraham was over 80 yrs. old and his close to 80 yr. old wife was barren. Now, without being patient Abraham

110

made a terrible mistake, Ishmael, his son from a maidservant. But when he got on track and began operating in patience, Abraham and Sarah had Isaac. By this time Abraham was 100 yrs. old and Sarah was close to 91 yrs. old.

God showed him a principle; a principle about speaking words of life, God called Abraham the father of many nations. God ushered this along by changing the man's name from Abram to Abraham, which means father of many nations. Abraham caught on to this principle and started calling things that weren't as though they were (Romans 4:17). So, Isaac was born after some time, Isaac had two sons, one of which had twelve sons, and that was Israel.

God has impressed this upon me so many times in my life. When I prayed for something, if it didn't come right away I would get impatient. But then God would tell me to be patient and it would come. I don't know why they didn't come right away but I don't care either. God would say, "I will give you (what you asked for), you just be patient and trust me." At first I thought that just meant wait but now I know that it means more than wait. Many of the things have not come yet and many have, but for those that have not I have His promise, His Word on it.

CALMNESS

Sometimes it is very hard to operate in patience. Believe me, I know how hard it is, especially when it came to my own physical health. When I saw other people get healed so fast it always made me so joyful. But then I looked at myself and I wasn't appearing physically healed yet, so I asked the Lord about it. I would say, "Why is my healing taking so long?"

I would preach on healing even if it never manifested, because it's in the Bible. Isaiah 53:5 tells us that we are healed now, it's a fact. So, as I mentioned before, the only things that will cause you to get sick are your knowledge of the Word, or lack of it, your confession of your mouth, anxiety (no use of patience), and not rightly discerning the body of Christ, or an attack of the devil. Satan will try to influence you into saying your sick but you don't have to say that. You can do what I do, you can confess what I confess over myself everyday. I always confess that I'm healed even if it doesn't look that way. Some people have said that healing had passed away, or it was only for the apostles or something totally off base and stupid like that. If you want to take up the argument that healing by God is outdated and passed away then all you have to do is prove that God has passed away or changed. Look at Hebrews 13:8.

Jesus tells us to believe we have received those things we asked for when we prayed and we shall have what we believed for (Mark 11:24). And we also read that

God wants us all well. Patience is of the fruit of the Spirit, which means if we are going to operate in the things of the Spirit then we must not forsake patience. It took a while, but through patience I can truly say that I'm healed. I never stopped confessing "I'm healed" even when I was on the floor dying, and my God came through.

FAITH AND PATIENCE

Hope is the blueprint that your faith builds upon and patience works right along with faith. Let's look at an example of a car for a minute. When you get in a car to go to the store (supposing the car is running) you have to steer that car or it will go off the road. Your faith is the car, and you have to steer it with your hope. Patience is the water or coolant to keep the car from over heating.

We see that faith and patience work together, and I'll tell you why. When you ask for something, anything according to His will, you must believe that you have received it. And you must use patience knowing that God is faithful and able to perform what He said He would (Jeremiah 1:12, Romans 4:21). If you are not patient, you are not going to get it from God.

People often say, "patience is a virtue." They are right, but it's not just a good moral, it's a must. James 1:2-3 tells us that trials and tribulations work patience. This

113

bears need for explanation or some people might get confused and I don't want that. We have patience simply because we are children of God, it was given to us when we were born again, but until there is a trial or tribulation it doesn't rise up within us. I said, in the previous paragraph, that patience works along with faith. One reason for this is because when we pray for something and it doesn't manifest right away we've got a trial on our hands. And if you don't have patience *and use it* you would blow your faith right out of the water because you would destroy your hope. As a result you would never get the manifestation, from God, of what you prayed for. Healing is the same way; if you went up for a healing prayer line and nothing manifested right away your patience has to spring into action or you never will get healed that way. Another reason for this is that some prayers take longer to manifest than others. I don't understand all the reasons why that would be, but …

Say, Jay prayed for a new house with no mortgage payments. That would take some time to manifest, especially when Jay is in the midst of a physical trial and he's on welfare with no job. Jay prays for physical healing for smaller things and they manifest faster; he prayed for financial security and he doesn't owe anyone anything and he would like to keep it that way. You see, his faith has to grow just as he has to grow. He has to be patient for all these things that he has prayed for or he will blow his faith, then he would have to start all over.

STABILITY

I prayed for a certain kind of car a while back and confessed for it and stood firm for it. Then my eyes started wandering and looking at other nice cars, and I started thinking, '*Maybe I should have prayed for that car instead*.' Well, what happened is, I didn't get anything. Why? Because my mind was wavering, consequently I wasn't acting in patience and I stopped my faith. So, now we see that a wavering mind is opposed to patience.

"That person should not expect to receive anything from the Lord. Such a person is double-minded and unstable in all they do," (James 1:7-8 NIV).

The subheading, in the Bible, for this section— where James 1:7-8 are—is 'True Religion Patient In Temptation' and it is basically talking about praying for wisdom, but these verses apply to any prayers.

CHAPTER 10
CATEGORY OF KINDNESS

If a person is walking in true love and representing Jesus the Christ as being alive today that person will know kindness and its inclusions.

SYNONYMS

Some synonyms for kindness are benevolence (which means a giver), beneficence, good nature, grace, humanitarianism (that's not humanism), charity (which means a helper), philanthropy, mercy, hospitality, and love. A good test of your hospitality is like the time when my friend was going through a much-needed change. He was being tempered by God and putting off some of those bad habits. The test came when he needed a place to stay and I had a small one bedroom apt., I let him stay with me and I had to put up with his habits. I knew those habits were going to change, but it took a long time to change. This, you can see, was a job for patience.

Some synonyms for philanthropy are good Samaritan, benefactor, and almsgiver. This is really something that most people don't realize about kindness and doing acts of kindness toward others. Before I looked up these words for the fruit I did not know giving was of the fruit of the Spirit. I knew that it was something I wanted to do, but I had no idea that it tied directly to the fruit. There's something else that ties into the fruit by way of giving and that is receiving. One of the synonyms of kindness is beneficence, which relates to being on the receiving end.

GIVING AND RECEIVING

There is a spiritual principle set up by God that says when you give, depending upon how your faith has grown, you can receive a hundred-fold. Besides that, when you give, I'm sure you realize that somebody has to receive. It is an act of kindness for you to give to the poor.

COURTEOUSNESS

There is another area of being kind that is not talked of in the synonym section of this chapter, but if you will act upon it you will understand it. It is called being courteous. In the Bible Jesus told a parable about the good Samaritan. He said that there was a traveler who was taking a far journey. On his journey he was attacked by some bandits. They left him half-dead and stripped him of all his possessions. Along came a priest whom, when he saw him, just passed by, then a Levite came and passed by on the other side when he saw him. However, when a Samaritan saw him he dressed and bound his wounds and took him on his own donkey to the nearest hotel, and took care of him. Then the Samaritan went to the innkeeper and told him to take care of the man, and said that if there were any added expenses that he (the Samaritan) would pay them upon his return. This parable Jesus told as an example of a neighbor, but it is also talking about being courteous to others. The dictionary says that a courteous person is marked by respect for and consideration for others. A synonym of courteous is gentlemanly, which goes back to being gentle (not brash or forceful) which means being kind.

What I see that this parable is saying about being courteous is that courteousness is a selfless act of kindness. When you walk down the street and see someone whom you can help, or when someone comes to you with a need and you can help them, don't be like that priest and that Levite, who just passed by on the other side. If you can do something to help, do something. That Samaritan was, according to many versions (and it would make sense), also going somewhere but he stopped and took the time to help this man, and paid for medical care for this stranger.

CHAPTER 11
CATEGORY OF GOODNESS

Goodness, as well as kindness, is a trait that is easily mimicked by unbelievers. If a person is walking in true love and representing Jesus the Christ as being alive today that person should know true goodness and its inclusions.

SYNONYMS

Here are some synonyms for goodness, so fasten your seat belts. First we find that excellence is goodness; to tell you the truth, that one just blew me away. Then I found merit, worth, virtue, and ethicality. The next word made me think a bit, it's honesty; and I thought, '*It's so sad to know that people who know how important honesty is lie anyway.*' I would ask someone to do something for me at such 'n' such a time, they said okay but when the time came they didn't do it. It meant something to me that they would do it but they just lied. Why did they lie? It was because they didn't want to hurt me by saying no; but they hurt me more by lying. Also, some people were raised to lie because they got lazy and their parents were liars. But they are humans, they aren't God.

Synonyms of honesty are integrity, veracity, honor, morality, scruples, sincerity, and good faith. Some people give their word but that doesn't mean a thing to them. Some people give their word and do their best to make good on their word but for some unforeseen reason they can't. When you give your word to someone do your best to make your word good—that makes your name good; if you can't do what you said you would do pick up the phone and call them. Don't leave them hanging, that may make them think that you are untrustworthy and you may loose a friend. Jesus never, in his whole life, said he would be somewhere and not show. Every time Jesus said he would go somewhere or do something, even every time he told someone he would be somewhere for them, he always kept his word. The Bible gives us many illustrations of this. Even at the tomb of Lazarus, Jesus said he would come, but he didn't give a time. Mary, Martha and the Jews that were there had to use faith and patience, but he came. I challenge you, do as Jesus did, be honest.

When a person tells you he will do something for you and doesn't do it, whether or not he meant to, he lied. Now, you should forgive him, but he just showed you that it could be risky to try and count on him. There is but one way that you can show anyone that you can be trusted and that is to hold to your words. Sometimes people make promises and then think, '*Oh, I wish I didn't do that.*' They try to ask the person if they could be released from their promise (be forgiven in advance). The other guy won't forgive them so they can either keep their word or try to lie about it (just not do it). This is not legalism, it's honesty. Here is what Jesus says about lying,

"You belong to your father, the devil, ... When he lies, he speaks his native language, for he is a liar and the father of lies," (John 8:44 NIV).

One time I saw a girl in my church who had no Bible, and I said to her, "I'm going to get you a Bible." I had no money but I was bound to that promise. So, with the $5 that I found packed away in my drawer, I went to a bookstore. All the Bibles there were $13 and up, all but one. A full Old and New Testament King James Bible, just one, was sitting there with no price on it. I brought it up to the desk and the man told me it was $2.50. This was in the later 80's when Bibles were $16.00 and up. God honors a man who will keep his word to do a kind act.

Here's a good illustration of lying: I'm sure you all know of the San Andréas Fault. Well the San Andréas Fault started a long time ago with one small crack in the ground. Now, let's compare that one small crack to one small lie, "Yes I brushed my teeth," when you didn't. Add another small crack, another small lie, and the gap gets larger; it gets harder to tell the truth. So we keep adding cracks and lies. Soon we have a wide chasm called the San Andréas Fault, and your name is ruined because of all the lies you have told. Now, the only way to rebuild a credibility rating is to learn how to catch yourself in your own lies and humble yourself enough to correct yourself *in front of the one you just lied to*. I know a guy who promised me a video card for my computer and then said, "Wait, let me make sure I have one so I don't lie to you."

REMEMBERING

Ya know, calendars are made to help you remember things. So, if you have trouble remembering something, don't let it turn into a lie, write it down on a calendar. Many people say, "Well, I have a good memory so I'll remember it," but they have the most problem with remembering the little things. For instance, when I went to the store I often forgot what I needed. But then I started making a list of what I needed, and had no problem remembering.

GOD'S WORD

Did you ever notice that Jesus always spoke honestly? Sure he had fun and probably joked around with his disciples, but he never said a word that wasn't in line with truth. As we found out, a synonym of goodness is veracity or verily which means truth or truly. Jesus always said, "Verily, verily, I say unto you ..." Well, we don't need to say verily, verily, but we can tell the truth. All we have to do is use God's Word when we speak, let God have your tongue.

GOD IS GOOD

Be good, exercise goodness, even as your heavenly Father is good. Doing as the Father does is doing good. God is good, and man (and woman) is made in the image and likeness of Him, we were made to be like He is. Remember, one of the synonyms of goodness is excellence, that's what we were made to be. So we were made good and then sin entered in. But just because sin entered into man does not mean we are all doomed to hell. There is a way, only one way of escape. Jesus is Lord and he will save you from sin, but you must confess him as Lord and believe what you say down in your heart. Then what you must do is do good. This is the way it is; the opposite of good is sin. If you don't think so ask God, ask Good. So, "Turn from evil and do good; seek peace and pursue it," (Psalm 34:14 NIV).

We see, in Proverbs. 3:27, that we have the capability to do good. If it were impossible to do so then God would not have told us, through Solomon, to do good. When someone does a good deed for you, you

125

repay him with good. But it isn't enough to repay good with good; in the Bible Jesus said to repay evil with good (Mathew. 5:44). You should be the first to do a good deed, it is written to do unto others as you would have them do unto you (Matthew 7:12). Jesus was God's man on the Earth; he represented Him as the good God that He is. You are God's man or woman on the Earth today; represent Him as the good God that He is.

When you go to the store to buy something, you take it to the clerk and pay for it. If you don't pay for it they won't let you have it. The payment is doing a good deed. When you go to a restaurant you order, they bring your food, then you pay your bill and usually leave a tip, that is doing good. When you go to church you sit there. What's wrong with that statement?

At the church (the local body) are they feeding you any spiritual food that's nourishing, anything you would care to eat? If you can eat some of the spiritual food that they have there then it would be good if you could pay for it, give an offering. This is not saying that you have to, but it would be good. If you are not getting anything out of it and they don't need you—some church bodies will say they need you only because you can give—it would be good to find a (local) church where you are being fed nourishing food and they need your talents. The body of Christ (the Church) needs everyone, everyone has a purpose in the body of Christ.

The apostle Peter tells us "how God anointed Jesus of Nazareth with the Holy Ghost and with power, who went about doing good, and healing all that where

126

oppressed by the devil, for God was with him," (Acts 10:38 KJV).

Is God with you, are you born again? If you are born again then God is with you so do good.

COPY OF GOD

"Then God said, 'Let us make man in our image, in our likeness, ...'" (Genesis 1:26a NIV). When God made man He made a duplicate of Himself, not as some religious denominations think. Many denominations make it sound like man was made to be some sort of sub-species, like a worm. There is a scripture verse that supports this idea when it is not studied out. That verse is Hebrews 2:7 (taken from the Old Testament, Psalms 8:5) and it is actually saying that God created man and put him (as a position of learning) lower than angels. Before we were born again, yes, we were lower (in learning) than angels but now that we are born again, legitimate children of God, we are no longer on a lower learning level. We should now know more than the angels. That is why this verse is true, "Are not all angels ministering spirits sent to serve those who will inherit salvation?" (Hebrews 1:14 NIV).

God made man to be His equal, His duplicate. He copied Himself. Adam could do everything that his Father could do. He was a good, honest, kind, thoughtful, faithful man and all the attributes of God operated in his live. God made Adam to be god of this Earth and to be so much like God that if you knew Adam you would not be able to tell the difference. When Adam was tempted he sloughed off his authority to the enemy. But, thanks be to God, Jesus came and got it back then gave it back to man, right where God intended it to be in the first place.

Another, probably a better, rendering of Psalms 8:5 (the verse that Hebrews 2:7 was taken from) is this, "You made him little less than God and crowned him with glory and honor," (Psalm 8:5 HCSB). When God copied Himself He wasn't crazy, He didn't think He was a worm so He didn't make man to be a worm. He had a purely sober image of Himself so He made man to be like that image. So, if you can find something in the Bible that tells you what God is like, you have just found something that tells you what you should be like too. Look at it like this: God is the original, an original masterpiece, and He put Himself through a copy machine and out came mankind. But the copies became foggy, the devil made sure of that, not ruined just foggy. So, God sent Jesus and the Holy Spirit to clean up those copies and get them back into focus.

CHAPTER 12
CATEGORY OF FAITHFULNESS

Faithfulness does not mean having faith. Fact is that there is no way you can really have faith in someone whom you are not being honest with. And honesty is part of faithfulness.

SYNONYMS

Some synonyms of faithful are fidelity, allegiance, confidence, loyal, true, and constancy. If you are an honest person—at least one who tries to be honest—and you make a promise to someone you ought to instill confidence in them, a reason for them to believe you. Some synonyms of true are actual, loyal, sincere, and straight. The way to instill confidence in the one you made the promise to is to be sincere and straight. Some synonyms of constant are unfailing, unrelenting, diligent, consistent, true, and loyalty. The word **true** is both a synonym and a definition of faithfulness. Before we can be true to others we must first be true to ourselves and to God. Consistent means to be always the same way meaning stay on the Word of God. Jesus, in his ministry, stayed on the Word, you will not find one place where Jesus ever swayed from the Word of God. When the devil came against him he didn't go into a fear fill fight, he just said, "It is written ..." (and told him what was written) and the devil could not stand in his way. Then the devil came back and said, in essence, why don't you do this because "It is written ..." and Jesus simply replied. "It is also written ..." So Jesus always stayed on the Word of God, and he never failed to come through on a promise. I don't make promises too much unless I know that I can make good on them.

Can I trust you? The best synonym for faithfulness is reliability, which means trustworthiness. Everywhere I go I might meet Christians who truly love the Lord. I ask them to call me or to write back to me and they tell me that they will. But when the time comes to do it I don't hear from them. I know they are still growing, as we all are, but that's no excuse for not being reliable. The best example of reliability is God and that example should be preached and taught in every church and everyone should pattern their lives after Him.

This goes right along with telling the truth. Now, God is truth and He is the Father of speaking words of truth and love. There are many people who want to be honest but they don't know, yet, the right words to say (they don't know how). So those people end up speaking words of death, which they think is the truth because that's what it looks like. But that's not the truth, God's Word is truth (John 17:17), and something that isn't God's Word (truth) is what?

What's something that's not the truth? Is it not a lie? Then what gives you the right to go around, as a Christian, speaking something that isn't in line with God's Word? So in the spiritual realm words of death (not life) are actually lies. It doesn't look like lying until you look at what God (truth) said, then you can see it for what it is. The true truth speaker is the one who lines his words up with the Word of God. On the other hand, Satan is the father of lies (John 8:44). You could fall into Satan's trap and not even know it until it's to late. The only way to keep yourself from falling into his trap is to be baptized in the Holy Spirit (1 John 4:1-4). That is only the first step but it is not all you can do. The next thing is to line up everything you say with the Word of God. When you get ready to speak you should ask yourself, "What would Jesus say in this instance?" If you don't know, beyond a shadow of a doubt, what He would say ask Him. It's just like when you have to react to something, you should first ask yourself, "What would Jesus do?" Again, if you don't know ask Him. The Holy Spirit is our guide through life and He will point out the pit falls.

Now, talking about speaking, I don't mean that you can only speak prophecy and what's written. But it would be a very good idea for us all to make it possible for anyone to read the Bible and logically reason why we said what we said.

131

BE YE FAITHFUL BECAUSE YOUR GOD IS FAITHFUL

Faithfulness is a major part of the fruit of the Spirit, which is love. Think about it, you want to be a good witness and lead other people to the truth of God's Word. But you just missed an important appointment. You said that you just forgot but truthfully you didn't go because you found something else that you just wanted to do then. Why didn't you at least call and cancel the appointment before hand and apologize for your actions. See, when you make an appointment to do something and you *purposely* forget about showing up without even telling the other person, you just lied to that person and proved yourself unfaithful. And so, you made yourself out to be a terrible representative of Jesus, whom you said you followed.

Now, I'm not trying to condemn anybody because I've done it too.

"When a man makes a vow to the Lord or takes an oath to obligate himself by a pledge, he must not break his word but must do everything he said," (Numbers 30:2 NIV).

Some people might say, "But I do most of it." And others might say, "I always tell people that I'll do more than I can actually do. And when the time comes to do it

I'm so swamped with so many things to do that I just can't do it all."

For that first excuse, the Bible doesn't say "do most of it and what you don't do say 'so what.'" It says to do everything you said you would do. Now, of course that's not talking about carrying out wicked and perverted actions like murder and sinful stuff like that. When you give your word that you will do an act of righteousness for someone at a certain time you had better do it at that time.

The second excuse is all to typical among outgoing, loving Christians; they want to do so much for everyone that they seem to over-extend themselves with doing good deeds. But the only way to help these people not to burn themselves out, and so they can do everything they said they would do is if they can cut down on giving their word that they will do all these things for everyone. I'm one of them so I know what I'm talking about. I find that it is very helpful to carry a day timer with you as you talk to people, then when they ask you to do something for them at a certain time you can look at your day timer and see if you have time to do it. Otherwise you will have to use that word that Christians don't like to say to anyone but the devil, "No."

Let me ask you this: have you ever had someone tell you that they would do something for you at a certain time and not come through? It hurt, didn't it? And it was something that would be very hard for you to do by yourself. But you needed it done because that was the first step in something that you were doing for someone else on a deadline. I realize that you must have felt very mad at that person. But you must forgive them because unforgiveness will kill you from the inside out. Besides, if you don't forgive that person then 9 times out of 10 you will wind up doing the same thing to someone you love.

So once you have forgiven that person who lied to you by making that promise to you and not fulfilling it then you can be honest by not breaking your word to someone else. Ya see, whether he is a believer or not Jesus died for him. Now, why should one person that Jesus died for be worthy of respect (honesty, truth, sincerity ...) and someone else whom Jesus died for not be worthy of the same respect just because one is a believer and the other isn't. We as Christians are born again to love, a life of love, we are supposed to win the lost to Christ. But we cannot do that if we lie to them or they see us lying to each other.

The Hebrew meanings for faithfulness are trusty, stability, steady, security, and continuance. By trusty the writer is saying; do you show that people can trust you? By stability and steady he is saying; don't say one thing to one person and another to another person. By security he's saying; can people trust your words? By continuance; tell the truth and stick with it.

"In love a throne will be established; in faithfulness a man will sit on it—one from the house of David—one who in judging seeks justice and speeds the cause of righteousness," (Isaiah. 16:5 NIV).

This is saying that the man or woman who will sit on the throne (reign in life) is to be one who is honest, stable—not wishy-washy—and will hold to the truth, and is to be a person that people can trust. Guess what. You are that man or woman, or you should be. Those who are in Christ are the seed of Abraham (Galatians 3:29). David was of Abraham's lineage; you know that because he was a Hebrew. And since the lineage of David was in the lineage of Abraham and Jesus was in the lineage of David then guess what. You and me, we are also in the lineage of David. And because, we know, Jesus is the One to sit on the throne and we are in Christ and joint heirs with Jesus we are sitting on the throne also. Please don't make a mockery of the throne by being unfaithful.

First, you have to forgive those who have wronged you in the past, that includes lying to you, and repent of wrongs you've done to others. And then you have to put away the past so that it does not have any effect on your future, any adverse effect. Then you have to make the proper adjustments so that you will not do them again. This may, and probably will, take time but you had better start now.

CONTRACTS

Let's talk for a bit about oral and written contracts; I took contractual law in college. A contract is basically an agreement between at least two parties, you and anyone (from God, Satan, the president ... all the way to your dog or cat) that is signed. The signing of the contract takes many forms, for an oral contract what's accepted in America is a handshake, for a written contract it's a signature. The signing of the contract makes it ironclad, and not one party can legally dissolve it. Let's first look at the oral contract.

Oral

An oral contract consists of promises and conditions just like a written contract. When it is signed by whatever means you choose (sometimes it's just a word "Okay") it's legal and binding, in a company of witnesses. If one party doesn't hold up to their end of the deal the contract is breached and proper measures can be taken. This too is legal enough to be taken to court, depending on the circumstances.

Example #1

Joe and Matthew went into a contract together, it was an oral contract. Joe needed someone to help him mow his yard—it was a big yard—and Matthew needed someone to weed his garden while he was on vacation. So they made an agreement that Matthew would help Joe with his lawn if Joe would weed Matthew's garden over vacation. The contract was signed by a handshake. When Matthew got home from vacation he found that his garden hadn't been weeded. He went over to Joe's house and asked him why he didn't fulfill his end of the bargain. Joe said, "I just forgot." Matthew told Joe that he would have to find someone else to help with his lawn then because the contract that they both signed was breached. Matthew was no longer obligated to fulfill his part of the deal.

Written

Written contracts are much the same as oral contracts, but in many cases they are more binding. A written contract is a tangible document with sections (called clauses) in it. A clause can take one of three forms; demands, promises, or promises with conditions. The promise with condition clause is always marked with the words 'if' or 'and' somewhere in the clause. The promise clause is marked with the words 'will,' 'shall' or 'going to' somewhere in it. When two or more parties sign this legal agreement they are saying that they agree to carry out everything written in it. A caption in the midst of a clause—we could call it an unless caption—is there in some clauses, if desired, for extenuating circumstances such as money problems. If one party keeps most of the contract but doesn't keep every clause written in it that party is breaching the contract, and appropriate measures can be taken. If there are three or more parties involved in the contract and one breaks his end then that one is in danger of being sued by both of the other two, but the other two (or more) must carry out the contract between the remaining parties.

Example #2

Joe's Building Contracting Company and Sam's Designers where contracted by Skyscrapers Limited to build a high rise in down town S.F. They signed the contract and started to work. After a few weeks Joe's found that it would cost a bit more money than expected, so they talked to the owner of Skyscrapers. Joe decides that he can't do the work so his company walks off the job. Well, this puts Sam in a pinch because he is still obligated to do his share. So Sam's and Skyscrapers are both (as a joint effort) going to take Joe's to court because of breach of contract. Joe's only excuse was that there wasn't enough money, but there was not a clause in the contract to give provision for that. This means big trouble for Joe's and it could wipe them out. But now Sam's has more work to do because they have to do alterations on this building and Sam's business is not a building contractors business. You see, if there isn't a caption for money concerns where money is a variable then money is not a reason for breaching a contract.

God's contract

But there is one form of contract (covenant) that is even more blinding than that and that is a blood covenant. If a blood covenant is breached the first party doesn't take the breaching party to court, they kill them. God made a blood covenant with us. God's covenant is actually a three-fold covenant, it is blood but it is also written down

138

for us to read (the Bible) and He also spoke it to us, so it's also oral. God signed this covenant (contract) we didn't, not until we (you now) make a firm commitment to keep His contract. Ya see, His ways are higher than our ways (Isaiah 55:9) and His way of operating this contract is not the way man would do it. If you break your end of the contract He will forgive you and let you back in the contract again if you ask Him.

Again I say, patience, peace, faithfulness and faith all work together and here is why. You see, we have faith (rely on, believe, obey, trust) in God because He is faithful (reliable and trustworthy) and we must use patience and peace to see the manifestation of the things He promised us. Suppose God said, for example, "You will have that new car that you prayed for." You have no legal or spiritual right to only be at peace and patient for that car the first month and then get anxious because it hadn't manifested yet. He didn't say anything about time. And if Jan tells you that she will be going to New York soon and you can go with her, don't get anxiety ridden if she doesn't go the next day. Don't stay home and miss all that's happening to wait for her to go. While the other person is being faithful to his or her promise, you should be at peace and patient for them, and for yourself.

God has given me a promise, a specific promise, something that I prayed about. But I have to be at peace and patient because it hasn't come manifested yet. God is working on me, bringing me into a position to receive the manifestations of all these things I prayed for. By my thanking Him all the time for the things I prayed for, although the manifestations aren't in yet, I am being patient and constantly on His Word, that's what He said to do. If He weren't faithful there would be no way I could be at peace and patience; this is because I couldn't trust Him.

CHAPTER 13
CATEHORY OF GENTLENESS

This is another thing that can be faked by unbelievers. The problem is that, besides the fact that they're not making an eternal difference, the unbelievers will not be able to carry it on forever, they have their limits.

SYNONYMS

Ready for some synonyms that will knock your socks off? Some synonyms of gentleness are mild, easy, moderate, and temperate. Just out of a desire to learn, I looked up temperate and temperance—the word used for self-control—in the King James Bible. The results of my search are very interesting and thrilling. This is what I found, temperate means moderate in appetite and desire, whereas temperance (self-control) means moderate in appetite and desire. They're the same, so gentleness includes kindness, goodness, meekness, and self-control.

Just to give you a little more knowledge about gentleness here are some synonyms of temperate. They are reasonable, sober, levelheaded, composed, collected, and pleasant. Have you ever been around people who always looked on the dark side of things whenever you saw them? It just seems that every time you saw them they always had a bad report, never had anything good to say. If they are born again they are just not walking in gentleness, or any of the fruit of the Spirit for that matter (walking in love). They just aren't walking in the light of what they have. They have a bad disposition because they are either carrying the cares of *whatever* or they are mad at something. They don't mean to be that way, they just don't know that there is a better way, or they are stuck in a rut from the old way of life. But if they are so hung up on the things of this world's system it will be very hard to turn them to see the truth, but not impossible.

CONFESSION

You have seen how a jeweler holds a woman's gold chain necklace or perhaps you have handled one yourself. If you have then you know that it's very fragile, very delicate. Well, so are people. You can ruin a man's life or add life to him with your tongue if that person chooses to receive from you. You can also ruin your own life or add life to your life. This goes along with James 3:7-8, which say,

"All kinds of animals, birds, reptiles and creatures of the sea are being tamed and have been tamed by man, but no man can tame the tongue. It is a restless evil, full of deadly poison," (James 3:7-8 NIV).

But God is not a man as we know man, He can tame your tongue. Another thing that it goes along with is the power of a positive confession. "Words kill, words give life; they're either poison or fruit—you choose," (Proverbs 18:21 MSG).

I'm sure you've heard of the power of positive thinking. I believe this is talking about thinking in your heart, believing, and that would make sense to what I'm about to say. That is great, you should think positively about everything, everybody and every situation. That is a great directive because Jesus did say that out of the abundance of your heart, those things that you are thinking down in your heart, your mouth speaks.

"You are a bunch of evil snakes, so how can you say anything good? Your words show what is in your hearts," (Matthew 12:34 CEV).

In other words, what's in your heart is what you are going to speak (and I don't mean what's in your thumper).

Don't get me wrong, I know that there are comedians who make jokes using bad confessions and

143

don't mean them but that has nothing to do with everyday life, it has nothing to do with you either. What I am saying is, when you think something bad about someone, or yourself, in your heart, you begin to speak it over and over, and you begin to dwell on it, then what started with a harmless though soon becomes a deadly situation. My friend, that is not advisable, it's sinful. Jesus said that if you speak it with your mouth and believe it in your heart then that is what will come to pass (Mark 11:23) let me quote that verse.

"For assuredly, I say to you, whoever says to this mountain, 'Be removed and be cast into the sea,' and does not doubt in his heart, but believes that those things he says will be done, he will have whatever he says," (Mark 11:23 NKJV).

There are many places in the Bible where God connects the tongue (speaking) to the heart (believing).

You are made by God, you are made to spread the good news. A confession of death (a negative confession) is not spreading God's Word (good news), indeed it's spreading Satan's word. But a confession of life is speaking God's Word. Your tongue has such great power to give life or death (Proverbs. 18:21a).

When Jesus appeared in the book of Revelations he had a sword coming out of his mouth that is sharper than any two edged sword. I believe that is to show two

144

things; first the Word of God (Ephesians. 6:17) and, second the power of life and death in the tongue.

"Words can bring death or life! Talk too much, and you will eat everything you say," (Proverbs. 18:21 CEV). What can be taken from that is that when a person keeps spouting out non-life giving words and talks poor health, poverty, low self esteem, and the like that person is indulging in the gift of the tongue in those areas. So, the fruit they will eat (reap) will be poverty, poor health, low self-esteem, and the like.

"You are a bunch of evil snakes, so how can you say anything good? Your words show what is in your hearts. Good people bring good things out of their hearts, but evil people bring evil things out of their hearts. I promise you that on the day of judgment, everyone will have to account for every careless word they have spoken. On that day they will be told that they are either innocent or guilty because of the things they have said, " (Matthew 12:34-37 CEV).

From these verses you can see how much importance God puts on the words that come out of your mouth. This is why I and many other preachers, and the Lord, stress a positive confession.

GENTLENESS OF THE APOSTLES

"But we were gentle among you, just as a nursing *mother* cherishes her own children," (1 Thessalonians 2:7 NKJV). Therefore, be gentle when you are among the brethren. But also be gentle among strangers and those who would persecute you. Don't be foolish, know what you are doing, but be gentle. Many times through your being gentle people can see that there is something different about you. And sometimes they can even see Jesus in you. I believe people could see Jesus in Paul; though Paul never met Jesus personally he portrayed Jesus in everything he did (after he was saved).

Look at Peter; Peter was a man who, before Jesus died, was an 'I can do it' type of man and a 'do it my way' man. But after Jesus died and Peter was baptized in the Holy Spirit he laid down his arrogance and took up Jesus' piousness. It was no longer Peter who was doing the works, when it was they were not great feats of wonder, instead it was Christ in him who did the miraculous things. If Peter and Paul and the others where alive today, and you met them, you would be thrilled to see Jesus in their faces and showing through their acts of gentleness. They patterned their lives after that of Jesus; that is what God is asking, rather telling, us to do.

DISCERNMENT

God also tells us to use discernment (which comes through the baptism in the Holy Spirit) when following orders of those in positions of authority. For example, if the president passes a law that tells us to disown Christ, we can't do that and you know that (that's clear). But if he passes a law that tells us to listen to all the news that floats around on the media, using discernment will tell us that we cannot follow that law because it is against the law of God. The bad news of this world will corrupt our minds.

"Finally, my friends, keep your minds on whatever is true, pure, right, holy, friendly, and proper. Don't ever stop thinking about what is truly worthwhile and worthy of praise." (Philippians 4:8 CEV).

DON'T BE RUDE

The Bible says that you can be gentle with those who are coarse with you. Be gentle and meek (humble) in the face of those who would persecute you and your enemies. You will change them by your actions, I know, it happened for me at work. When I first started working there, there was a guy who was very difficult, especially when he found out that I was a born again Christian. When I was operating in gentleness he seemed to get worse. Then he got better and I was noticing great changes taking place in him. He even apologized to me once. I know why this happened and it wasn't just some earthly reason, it was because I was operating in gentleness and refused to be rude. That is how the Holy Spirit operated in this case.

WISDOM

"But the wisdom that is from above is first pure, then peaceable, gentle, easy to be entreated, full of mercy and good fruits, without partiality, and without hypocrisy," (James 3:17 KJV).

If you are not operating in gentleness, no matter what you think about wisdom, you're not being wise to heavenly things. But, being gentle is not the only quality of wisdom, you must operate in peace, gentleness, meekness, fairness, and you must keep to the Word of God. Be gentle to others as your heavenly Father is gentle with you. The wisdom from worldly man (natural wisdom) is sensual and is led by their emotions, by their desires, by the situations around them and by what other

148

people say. Its worldly wisdom that's to blame for most, if not all, of the unwed mother cases and the abortion cases, because worldly wisdom doesn't tell you to use foresight. In these cases you (the person) are led by nothing more than immediate situational desires. This can, and usually is, very dangerous because, for one thing, abortion is murder, and sickness can have a festival. AIDS can spread like melted butter and Sodom (that ancient sin city) will emerge from its ashes.

SENSITIVITY

One other area of being gentle is being sensitive to the needs and problems of others. This goes along with an area of kindness called being courteous to others. Sensitivity is also an area of goodness. There are plenty of Scriptures in the Bible on these two areas but they don't use the two words **sensitive** and **courteous** in them. One Scripture is Luke 6:6-11 about the man with the withered hand. The Pharisees and Sadducees were not sensitive to the need, they were caught up in the fact that it was done on the Sabbath. I don't believe that it's because something good happened that the Pharisees and Sadducees were mad, although that may also have crossed their religion. I believe that the Pharisees and Sadducees were just brought up with the idea that miracle healings were constituted as work and that couldn't be done on the Sabbath. In other words, what Jesus was doing was unlawful in their eyes. This happened many times in the Bible; and being insensitive is not just isolated to the gospels. Jesus said, "You strain out a gnat (you look for the minor things) and you swallow a camel (you miss the major things)" (Matthew 23:24). A miracle happened and a man got healed, and they could only see that he did it on the Sabbath.

CHAPTER 14
CATEGORY OF SELF-CONTROL

Self-control is something that everyone, whether Christian or not, needs to operate in; although it seems pretty clear, by looking at people's lives, that self-control is not widely practiced. And although everyone needs it, there is only one true source. Unbelievers are just operating in a placebo, a faked self-control. I say that because self-control is more involved than meets the eye; indeed, all of the fruit of the Spirit is.

SYNONYMS

I went over and looked at the synonyms for self-control. And this is what I found; self-control is the same as self-discipline, self-constraint, composure, constraint, reserve, austerity, temperance, and (hold onto your hats) prudence. Now let me give you some definitions of prudence. They are, from the Hebrew; wisdom, subtlety, discretion, knowledge, understanding, and sense. In the Greek they are insight and intellect. So when you are in an impulsive position where you feel great emotion, and you desire something or someone, I encourage you to use great discretion. Not the discretion of the world, which in many cases causes heart aches, but true godly discretion, which causes joy to rise up.

Here are some synonyms of temperance, which also means self-control. They are moderation (sobriety), conservationism, and prudence. Prudence, in the book of Proverbs, is often talked about in opposition to foolishness. God says that the foolish destroy themselves by the wild way they act, but then He says that the prudent do righteous things and, therefore, find life.

"An evil man is held captive by his own sins; they are ropes that catch and hold him. He will die for lack of self-control; he will be lost because of his great foolishness," (Proverbs 5:22-23 NLT).

LEARNING SELF-CONTROL

This aspect of the fruit of the Spirit is most vital to your personal well-being. However, it's the one thing everyone has the most trouble with. There are two kinds of self-control, there is the self-control of this world system and there is true self-control, which I call Holy Spirit-control. Everyone, whether born again or unbeliever, needs to learn and operate in one form of self-control or another. But there is only one teacher, unbelievers have to learn it by trial and error really.

Actually, everyone teaches a form of what they are calling self-control, but you still have to learn it by yourself.

For those who are born again and baptized in the Holy Spirit, He is our teacher and He can teach true self-control since He invented it. He is really the only one on the face of this planet who can correctly teach self-control (Holy Spirit-control, which is simply yielding your self to the Holy Spirit).

You really need to learn to operate in self-control, just like you need to learn to operate in goodness, kindness, patience, faithfulness, and gentleness and the rest of the fruit. But how can you learn the right way without a teacher? The Holy Spirit baptism takes care of that, the thing you have to do, assuming that you have accepted the Holy Spirit, is to do what He says.

GLUTTONY

Let's talk about an area of self-control which concerns weight gain and lose. Let's say you were in a restaurant and they wheeled the cart with all the delectable chocolate, and other flavor, cakes and cookies beside you, and said, "Would you like a desert, it's free with what you ordered." You may have a hard time, especially since you are on a diet. Some people might just do a Garfield and dive right in, and regret it later. On the other hand some people who are learning self-control and are of stronger wills might have to think twice and tell the waiter to get them away so as not to tempt them any further. However, the one operating in Holy Spirit-control, the one who is yielded to the Holy Spirit, will automatically say, "Thanks but no thanks."

When I go into a restaurant, for example, I automatically put a limit on how much I am going to eat. It's just like when I am fasting, I set it down, make an iron clad statement, to let myself and the devil know that I am not going to let any food go into my mouth from such time as I start until I stop. The Holy Spirit helps me to stay honest and I am determined to keep my word, so the devil has no grounds.

This can also affect under weight people. One time, a long time ago, I came home from the hospital and I was 121 pounds, I am 6 feet tall and if you know anything about medical science, that is way under weight. So, I said to God "I've got to gain weight," and I started eating like a horse. I wasn't gaining an ounce and I couldn't understand why because I was eating so much. But I was doing something, I was making myself sick. Then God spoke to me one day while I was sitting down, He said, "Your being a glutton." Well that, kind of, set me back in my seat. He told me to let Him take care of the weight and He did. I stopped eating like a horse and a short time later I weighed 155 lbs., right where I wanted to be. Gluttony just happens to be one thing that Sodom (that ancient sin city of the Bible) was accused of. "Sodom's sins were pride, gluttony, and laziness, while the poor and needy suffered outside her door.' (Ezekiel 16:49 NLT).

Here is another example from my own life. Another time when I was in the hospital my mother went out and bought me an Angel Food cake, that is my favorite desert; I also had a bunch of cookies on my table right in front of me. Then my doctor came in and told me that I couldn't have them, that I was to be put on a no food diet, but he didn't take them away. I thought to myself as I looked at all the goodies, *'I can't have this. Well, I'll just have to find someone to take it then so it doesn't go to waist.'* A short while later my nurse came in and, knowing that the doctor had just taken me off all food and seeing that cake and those cookies in front of me, asked me how I could just sit there with all that food around me. I looked at her and said, "I know a bit about self-control," of coarse, I meant Holy Spirit-control.

Now let me tell you about a problem area that is common. You know about the common problem of being over weight. You say, "I have a weight problem." There is weight involved with the problem, but it springs from something else. It is either a food problem, which, if you dig down deep, is actually a lack of self-control where food is concerned, not knowing how to operate it, or a malfunction of the body. If it is a malfunction of the body God will heal your body.

If it's a food problem, a lack of self-control where food is concerned, learn self-control in dealing with food and exercise, repent of what you were doing to the temple of the Holy Spirit and watch the pounds fall off. Stop sinning against your own body; it looks like you would have more sense than that. There is a manual to true self-control, just like there is a manual to life, it's called the Bible.

ADDICTIONS

"My people are destroyed from lack of knowledge ..." (Hosea 4:6a NIV). In most cases the world's system has taken a lack of self-control and called it addiction. An addiction is a chemical dependency that can have adverse effects on you in the areas of your physical and mental health. And to make matters worse they say that you can never be cured from it, you can only be "recovering."

A while ago I was on an addictive drug—by doctor's prescription—and it was having adverse affects on me, physically, but I didn't understand that I was addicted. When it was revealed to me that I was addicted I went to my doctor and told him that I wanted off that addictive drug. The thing about that kind of drug, as the doctor says, "If you come off it all the sudden it could have negative side affects, it could kill you."

It is not God's will that you suffer with sickness and disease, my friend. He gave the knowledge to the doctors (et al) so that during the manifestation period of your health you can be comforted.

My friend, to be told you have to go through life as a "recovering" something and never to be cured (healed) is to be told a lie. Come to Jesus and be healed. As in the case of the alcoholic, the alcohol has an

156

addictive effect on the mind and body. But beer, wine, and most alcohol are not prescription drugs. This is just like any other addiction that starts by a lack of self-control. And the world's system says you can never be cured of this "disease," you can only go to clinics or a religious group and become a "recovering alcoholic' for life.

First of all, the word **disease** tells me that you can be healed because Jesus took up our infirmities and carried our diseases (Matthew 8:17). Secondly, although a disease may spring from alcoholism, the alcoholism is not a disease, if it were you couldn't stop drinking or you would die. I know men who have been totally set free from this addiction. Some people might say "Yeah, but that's only until they are offered a drink or they smell the alcohol." No!! The desire has been taken away when the addiction was taken away. The difference is that the world's system that says you will always be "recovering" teaches you how to combat the desire, whereas in the heavenly system the desire is taken away. The first way, where they taught you how to battle the desire is worldly self-control. The second way, where the desire is taken away, is Holy Spirit control, you gave it to the Holy Spirit.

You have a choice, either you can believe the trash about recovering and never being cured that you hear from the world's system, or you can look to Jesus and believe what he says, that you can be set free and healed. God led me to read Hosea 4 again and this stuck out at me, "Promiscuity, wine, and new wine take away [one's] understanding," (Hosea 4:11 HCSB).

"My people are destroyed for lack of knowledge," (Hosea 4:6). We could just as easily say that God's people, indeed all people, are destroyed because of a lack of self-control. God is saying that His people, all people, are destroyed because they don't know or even try to know the truth of the matter, they just go by what the world says about it. Look, God made the earth and everything and everyone in it, so who is man to think they can make the rules. When someone has a problem let him or her consult the One who formed the body, not some man who thinks he knows because he was taught by some man who was taught by some man ... who dreamed it up. God knows what is in man better than man does, after all He created man.

"For the god of this world has blinded the unbelievers' minds (that they would not discern the truth) ..." (2 Corinthians. 4:4a). Lies are more readily believed than truth and that is why there are so many professing "recovering addicts" and "recovering alcoholics" around. Because I never was an alcoholic, some people that know me would say to me, "Man, how would you know?" I know by the Holy Spirit of God, I also know a lot of people who were saved when they were alcoholics and are not alcoholics anymore. That verse, from the Living Bible, says, "Satan, who is the god of this evil world, has made him blind ...." In John 8:44 Satan is called the father of lies, Jesus said there is no truth in him. Another verse of Scripture says "let God be true, but every man be a liar ..." (Romans 3:4). So if you don't have documented evidence from God, if it's not written or backed up in the Bible, you're acting like a fool if you believe it—if it's
158

something someone calls a truth. That's why when God said, "My people are destroyed from lack of knowledge," He just as easily could have said, and maybe did say "My people are destroyed because they listen to the lies of this world instead of my truth."

Don't just think that someone who has had the same problem as you is right just because they say so. And just because there are books written on the subject doesn't mean they're right either. There is only One who is right, and that's God, and He is the only One whom you should believe. If you don't get God's Word on it to confirm it why should you believe it?

The spirit of alcoholism is brought on by a lack of self-control. And while the person is drinking his liver is being deteriorated and other problems can arise while the person drinks his life away. But the root of the problem is a lack of self-control, it has nothing to do with peer pressure; they can influence you to drink, but it's still your choice. It's just like when you plant a seed and that seed turns into a tree. Now you've got a tree of problems that started from a seed of a lack of self-control. You can't demolish that tree by changing that seed, you can't even find that seed anymore. But, you can take all the rest of that bad batch of seeds and exchange them for good seeds, and you can curse that tree and watch it die, (Matthew 21:19). It's purely your own fault if you are addicted to anything, excepting for when it's a doctor's prescription, then it's a joint venture. The spirit of alcoholism can be driven out, but the drinker must will it to be gone.

TRUTH VS. LIES

Brothers and sisters in Christ, and you who are still outside, the world will lie, cheat, and do whatever they can to keep you from getting more knowledge and power than they. Matthew 23:13 tells us that the religious systems of this world will shut the door to the kingdom of heaven in men's faces. Because of fear and other things they won't enter and they won't let others enter who see that that's a good place to go. These are religious preachers who are still in the world's system or maybe born again and just ignorant of the truth. This is a world that does not want you to get ahead, and if they think something otherwise from what you found out from the Bible then you're wrong. This is because they are afraid of being left behind or being moved from their comfortable position. This is even true where born again, Spirit filled Christians are concerned, if you say something that they don't believe that you're wrong—even if you can back it in the Bible—and up goes their defense. They don't like change and what you're saying means change. You had better have Scriptural evidence, use the Bible.

A SELF-CONTROL FAULT-LINE

Now, where there is a physical attraction between a man and a woman you might run into a self-control fault-line. This is where self-control is not strong consequently it falls away. And if you are "just friends" you could loose your friend that way. Or, if you are trying to witness to that person, a lack of self-control is a terrible witness. This is a definite place where you need self-control.

WALLOWING IN THE MUD

Before you read this chapter you probably thought as I did that everyone has their point where self-control falls away, along with all the fruit, because the person can't take it anymore, and he or she would just "wallow in the mud" for a while. Well, my friend, I've got some very good news for you, Jesus never wallowed in the mud. Oh, sure he had plenty of opportunities, but he never gave up, he just stayed right on with Holy Spirit-control. God had set down a pattern of living in His Word and then said to us, "If Jesus could do it you can do it through him." So when you're having trouble with self-control, or even when you're not, keep you're eyes on Jesus and take his example. When the temptations of the world came against Him, and they never failed to come against Him, He just turned to the Word.

"Imitate God, therefore, in everything you do, because you are his dear children. Live a life filled with love, following the example of Christ. He loved us and offered himself as a sacrifice for us, a pleasing aroma to God," (Ephesians 5:1-2 NLT).

CHAPTER 15
NOT MUCH TIME

How much time do you think you have? In truth, you don't have as much as you might think. You may have read this book, well, up to this point at least, and figured, "I don't have to even think about Jesus right now. I know that I need to get born again, but I have plenty of time, I'm only 12 years old." Congratulations, your 12; but now I've got a good question for you. Who guaranteed you that you will have another day on earth? "But I'm having so much fun now." Great. Do you think you can have more fun living as a sinner than living for Jesus? How do you know?

Ya see, right now you are basing your life, your fun, and everything else on what others have said. And those people might not, and probably don't, have your eternal fun life in mind. You can have just as much fun on earth living for Jesus as you can living as a sinner, maybe even more fun.

So, am I trying to influence your decision to live for Jesus? As a man of God it is my job; in other words, yes. So, yes, you will exist forever and ever, even after your life on earth is over; but where will that existence be? Will it be a true fun life in heaven with Jesus, or will it be an existence of sheer pain and pain upon pain in the place where Jesus isn't?

What if—

"Oh great, here he goes with the 'What if' questions."

Yes. What if you found out that you had two years to live; exactly two years to the minute? What would you do about Jesus?

You might say, "Well, I would live life to the fullest. Then one minute before I died I would accept Jesus as Lord. That way I wouldn't have to obey Him all my life."

You make it sound like obeying Him is a bad thing. Well then, what if you found out that you had exactly two days to live? What would you do about Jesus?

You might say, "I'd get so drunk that you would stop asking me these dumb questions."

You'd get drunk so that I would ... Think about how dumb that remark was. No, don't waste your time. Now, what if you found that you had only two seconds? What w—

By this time you might get upset and say to me, "Ha! You don't know how long I have to live, nobody really does—not even doctors—so stop asking me these dumb questions."

You just made my point. You don't know how long you have on this earth, so it looks like you—being a smart person—would do right by God before it's too late. You might not have another chance. Pray and confess this right now,

Dear God, in Jesus' name,

I now realize that my life has been getting me nowhere, nowhere in truth.

What the writer said is true, I don't know when my time on earth will end.

I'm declaring Jesus the Christ as my personal Lord now and I repent of sin.

I'm going to get a Bible and read it to find out what you want me to do, I don't want to be a hypocrite.

Thank you, Jesus, for saving me and showing me how to get to heaven.

It is my job to do what it takes to tell you the truth and influence your decision, but I can not—and I'm not allowed to even if I could—make that decision for you. As a counselor, my friend told me that people would ask him what they should do. He said that he might loose his license if he told a client what to do and it turned out wrong; he would be blamed and may end up in jail. He said that he could only tell them what he would do in the same situation. He said, "Because we are all different. They are not me and I am not them."

So, I can tell you that this is what I would do, to me it's a no brainer. But, this choice is up to you, either you will see Jesus as the truth and obedience to Him as Lord of your live as the right thing to do, or you won't.

FREE TO CHOOSE

Before you had accepted Jesus as Lord by a faith filled confession you had a choice.

"I call heaven and earth to witness this day against you that I have set before you life and death, the blessings and the curses; therefore choose life, that you and your descendants may live," (Deuteronomy 30:19 AMP).

But, you didn't have Jesus to run interference. Now that Jesus has come and defeated the devil *on his own turf* He has made it possible for you to call on Him and He will run interference for you.

Take an example from football: you are the quarterback but there is one problem—this is before you are saved—you are out there alone against the opposing team. Now that you are saved and Jesus is your Lord you have a team to run interference for you against the opposing team.

"But I thought that whatever happened to me was the will of God; that's what my pastor said," someone might say. Well, he was misled into thinking that himself by someone who was misled into thinking that, and the cycle goes on and on. If you will take a step back and analyze that statement and compare it with what Jesus said in the Bible you will find that it just doesn't hold water. It's a statement that started with the devil (the great deceiver), probably at the same time when he started the notion that the devil is dead and does not exist. I heard a song a while ago that said, I don't remember the words to quote it, that the devil was saying something like, *they don't believe that I exist anymore so now I can do things to them and they will think that it's God's will.*

"So, now that I made the choice to receive Jesus as Lord, what do I have to choose between? I thought that was it," someone may ask. Well, Proverbs says that life and death are in the power of the tongue. It's great that you chose life. Do you still have a tongue? In truth, Jesus said,

"The upright (honorable, intrinsically good) man out of the good treasure [stored] in his heart produces what is upright (honorable and intrinsically good), and the evil man out of the evil storehouse brings forth that which is depraved (wicked and intrinsically evil); for out of the abundance (overflow) of the heart his mouth speaks," (Luke 6:45 AMP).

So, it is really the heart that issues life or death. So, after you got born again and made Jesus your Lord by a faith filled confession did God remove your heart (spirit), and along with your spirit would go your character and personality and much, much more? You cannot live without your spirit. In other words, now that you are born again are you in heaven?

"No," you say. Well, in that case you still have choices to make every day. Have you ever heard of sin? That's something many people think should be preach to the unbeliever and not in church. And because it is preached in church, if it is, the born again people think that they must still be sinners. No, the choice to stay away from sin should be preached in church, and that message should be preached to those who have accepted Jesus. To the outsider maybe you should center up on what Jesus had done for them. Born again confessing Christians are not sinners,

"Therefore if any person is [ingrafted] in Christ (the Messiah) he is a new creation (a new creature altogether); the old [previous moral and spiritual condition] has passed away. Behold, the fresh and new has come!" (2 Corinthians 5:17 AMP).

168

But, just because you have made that choice to accept Jesus as Lord by your faith filled confession doesn't mean that you're in and you have no more choices to make. No, you have choices to make every day, not limiting it to dinner, clothes, and all that natural stuff. You now have the same choice from Deuteronomy 30:19, but you now have Jesus to run interference.

Before you accepted Jesus the devil had direct influence over you, you could not choose life unless a Christian or the influence of a Christian, a Christian book or a tract or movie or whatever, was present. Now that you have accepted Jesus, the influence of the devil is still there; but it is not direct, it is blocked by Jesus.

THINK ABOUT THESE THINGS

What you did yesterday may not have anything to do with what will happen tomorrow. I say **may** because if you lived as a sinner yesterday and you do nothing to the contrary today your sinful life will still effect your tomorrow. But, if you were a sinner yesterday, and today you repented of that life style and accepted Jesus' way, tomorrow will be so much brighter.

Normally, the law of time is that your yesterday cannot effect your tomorrow. What you do today effects your tomorrow. Allow me to clear that up; what you did one second ago has little to nothing to do with what happens in one second from now, it depends upon what you do now, this very second.

A friend said it this way, "The past is dead time and tomorrow never really comes, so all you have to operate in is now. So, what are you going to do?"

It looks to me like you have a choice to make. The choice is; who are you going to make your Lord? Will it be Jesus, your job, money, … what?

In closing this book I want you to think about three major things; Time, Choices, and Jesus.

BOOKS QUOTED FROM

www.ingramcontent.com/pod-product-compliance
Lightning Source LLC
Chambersburg PA
CBHW061722020426
42331CB00006B/1050